A Practical Guide to Fostering Law

by the same author

The Social Worker's Guide to Children and Families Law
Lynn Davis
ISBN 978 1 84310 653 1

See You in Court
A Social Worker's Guide to Presenting Evidence in Care Proceedings
Lynn Davis
ISBN 978 1 84310 547 3

of related interest

A Short Introduction to Attachment and Attachment Disorder
Colby Pearce
ISBN 978 1 84310 957 0

Nurturing Attachments
Supporting Children who are Fostered or Adopted
Kim S. Golding
ISBN 978 1 84310 614 2

A Practical Guide to Caring for Children with Attachment Difficulties
Chris Taylor
ISBN 978 1 84905 081 4

Understanding Looked After Children
An Introduction to Psychology for Foster Care
Jeune Guishard-Pine, Suzanne McCall and Lloyd Hamilton
Foreword by Andrew Wiener
ISBN 978 1 84310 370 7

Fostering A Child's Recovery
Family Placement for Traumatized Children
Mike Thomas and Terry Philpot
Foreword by Mary Walsh
ISBN 978 1 84310 327 1
Delivering Recovery Series

Just Care
Restorative Approaches to Working with Children in Public Care
Belinda Hopkins
Foreword by Jonathan Stanley
ISBN 978 1 84310 981 5

A PRACTICAL GUIDE TO

Fostering

Fostering Regulations,
Child Care Law and
the Youth Justice
System

Law

Lynn Davis

Foreword by Christopher Simmonds

Jessica Kingsley Publishers
London and Philadelphia

First published in 2010
by Jessica Kingsley Publishers
116 Pentonville Road
London N1 9JB, UK
and
400 Market Street, Suite 400
Philadelphia, PA 19106, USA

www.jkp.com

Library of Congress Cataloging in Publication Data
Davis, Lynn, 1962-
A practical guide to fostering law : fostering regulations, child
care law and the youth justice system / Lynn Davis.
    p. cm.
Includes index.
ISBN 978-1-84905-092-0 (alk. paper)
1. Foster home care--Law and legislation--England. 2. Foster children--
Legal status, laws, etc.--England. 3. Foster home care--Law and legislation-
-Wales. 4. Foster children--Legal status, laws, etc.--Wales. I. Title.
KD3305.D378 2010
344.4203'2733--dc22

2010006892

British Library Cataloguing in Publication Data
A CIP catalogue record for this book is available from the British Library

ISBN 978 1 84905 092 0

Printed and bound in Great Britain by
MPG Books Group

Acknowledgements

I am grateful to Ian Dixon of Chrysalis Care, Paul Corner of Nexus Fostering, Steve Bromage and the foster carers of By the Bridge and Nick Markendale for their helpful comments on the manuscript of this book. I hope they will find the finished version useful.

I am also grateful to Medway Youth Court for allowing me to observe proceedings.

Thanks go to Mum, Mark and the pack for their support and encouragement.

This book is dedicated to Nigel and Steffi.

Contents

ACKNOWLEDGEMENTS   5

Foreword   9

PREFACE   11

Introduction   13

Part I: Agencies and Carers   **15**
1.   Foster Care and Fostering Agencies   17
2.   Becoming a Foster Carer   25
3.   Placements   40
4.   Carers' Rights, Allegations and Ending Fostering   48

Part II: Fostered Children and Child Care Law   **63**
5.   Basics of Child Care Law   65
6.   Looked After Children   75
7.   Care Proceedings   86
8.   The Foster Carer as Witness   99
9.   Duties towards Looked After Children   111
10. Contact   128

Part III: Fostered Children and the Criminal Law   **137**

11. The Criminal System – Some Legal Basics   139
12. The Criminal Process   148
13. Reprimands, Warnings and Court   161
14. Sentencing   171
15. Anti-Social Behaviour   186
16. Young Victims and Witnesses – Evidence and Compensation   191

Part IV: Long-Term Plans   **207**

17. Long-Term Placements   209
18. Moving to Independence   217

JARGON BUSTER   224

RESOURCES   233

INDEX   236

Foreword

The family justice system is an ever-changing landscape, in which foster carers play a vital role. As a specialist child care solicitor and now as a District Judge, I have often seen the enormous contribution foster carers make to children's protection and the promotion of their welfare.

Foster carers are the ones on the ground, doing the day-to-day work with looked after children and dealing every day with the consequences of child abuse and neglect. Yet they are sometimes overlooked and undervalued as professionals in the world of child care. This book makes a significant contribution towards giving foster carers the knowledge and information they need to claim their rightful place as the backbone of the care system. It provides an important overview of the legal processes and principles underlying their role. It gives solid practical guidance and is written in Lynn Davis's customarily readable, accessible and helpful style. It is an essential read for anyone who is, or is considering, fostering and those who work with them. I am delighted to endorse it.

Christopher Simmonds
District Judge
Principal Registry of the Family Division
July 2010

Preface

I worked with foster carers when working as a child care lawyer for the local authority or for young clients, and in recent years I have given legal training courses to foster carers. I am full of admiration for their warmth and dedication. These days ever more demands are placed on foster carers, yet they are not always fully included in the professional team. Carers need to claim their place as key professionals in a legally complex field. They need the knowledge to do it. I hope this book will be a clear and practical guide to the main elements of the law surrounding foster care. A book can never be a substitute for legal advice on a particular case but at least it can provide a framework so carers are alert to legal issues and know when there is a question to be asked.

This book is up to date as of July 2010. However, the law is constantly evolving and it is always best to check that there have been no changes since publication.

In law, much as teenagers might not like it, the term 'child' applies to everyone until the age of 18. In this book, rather than laboriously using 'child or young person' all the time, I generally use one or the other. In the section about youth justice I refer to 'young person' because by definition we are talking about children over ten, but in the rest of the book I generally use the term 'child'. Unless specified, that includes everyone up to the age of 18 and I mean no disrespect to young people towards the upper end of the age range.

To avoid constant repetition of 'he or she', I have used both on different occasions. Unless it is clear from the context, everything applies equally to both sexes.

The book covers the law in England and Wales (the Scottish legal system is very different). In general, statutes apply to both countries equally, whereas regulations and guidance are usually similar but slightly different. I have tried to be clear where a legal provision applies only to one nation or the other, but, if nothing is specified, it applies to both.

Introduction

As a foster carer, you work in a highly regulated field, with laws, rules, regulations and guidance at every turn; laws governing you as a carer and the agency you work for, child care laws affecting the children you care for and when they move on and, for some, possible involvement in the criminal system.

This book is an attempt to help you find your way through the legal maze, become familiar with the jargon and specialist terminology, and understand the roles of the various people involved with your fostered child.

Understanding the legal framework will empower you as a foster carer and help you to claim your rightful place as one of the key professionals in the lives of the children you care for.

Part I
Agencies and Carers

Chapter 1

Foster Care and Fostering Agencies

What is foster care?

Foster carers are many and varied:

- Ann looks after babies for a local authority, moving them on to adoption.

- Barry cares for teenagers, moving them on to independence.

- Carol and David provide short-term placements for children removed in emergencies.

- Ed and Finbar care for a child long term.

- George works for an independent agency as a specialist remand foster carer.

- Hannah works for a charitable agency providing short breaks for children with disabilities.

- Ida provides therapeutic fostering for children with highly challenging behaviour.

- Jasmina looks after her niece under an Interim Care Order (ICO).

Their specialisms and day-to-day experiences are different, but they are all covered by the same rules and regulations. All are foster carers and the children they care for are among the 50,000 who are fostered in the UK on any one day.

Private foster care

Lucy needs someone to look after her daughter Mary full time. She does not approach the local authority, but just advertises for a carer. Nellie responds and the two women sort out arrangements, including payment, between themselves.

Nellie is a private foster carer. She has not been assessed or approved by a fostering agency and Mary is not a 'looked after child'. The local authority is only involved after the arrangement has been made, in order to ensure that it is suitable and to monitor the situation. Nellie's situation is legally very different from that of an approved foster carer.

The rest of this book concerns only approved foster carers for children looked after by local authorities.

Professionalism

Fostering has changed enormously over recent years. Being nice people with a spare bedroom is no longer enough: foster carers now play an ever more complex professional role with increasing demands placed upon them 24 hours a day, 7 days a week. They are increasingly recognised as an essential part of the children's workforce.[1]

However, unlike other child care professionals, foster carers look after vulnerable children in their own homes so we must have absolute faith in what goes on behind closed doors. For this reason, fostering is tightly regulated and a complex web of laws and regulations surrounds the children they look after.

What is fostering?

First, a question of terminology. The Children Act 1989 (henceforth referred to as CA89)[2] and some other legal provisions use the term 'foster parent'. However, 'foster carer' is now generally preferred as better reflecting the role, and that is the term used in this book.

---

1   See, for example, 'Options for excellence', Department of Health (2006). Available at www.dcsf.gov.uk/everychildmatters/resources-and-practice/RS00025, accessed on 4 July 2010.

2   In s23 CA89. Available at www.opsi.gov.uk/acts/acts1989/ukpga_19890041_en_1, accessed on 4 July 2010.

There is no single legal definition of fostering but we can infer the following key elements:

- Foster carers look after children who are not their own and for whom they do not have parental responsibility (PR) – fostering is all about looking after someone else's children.

- Foster carers care for children who are looked after by local authorities.

- They do so in their own homes as part of a family, not in an institution – there are normally no more than three unrelated fostered children in one home (so that it does not become like a children's home) and carers must agree to look after fostered children as if they were their own.

- It is a temporary arrangement (albeit sometimes a long-term one) always subject to review, unlike the permanence of adoption.

- The agencies involved, not the court, decide which child is placed with which foster carers.

Legal provisions

Fostering is one of the placement options available to local authorities for looked after children under CA89 (along with other possibilities like placement with parents or in children's homes).

Fostering agencies are governed by the Care Standards Act 2000 and the detail is filled in by the Fostering Services Regulations 2002 (as amended in 2008 and 2009) for England and the Fostering Services (Wales) Regulations 2003[3] for Wales (together known in the rest of this chapter as the 'Regulations'). Acts and Regulations lay down the law and must be obeyed. Agencies have to keep up to date with the law when new statutes and Regulations come into force, such as the Care Planning, Placement and Case Review (England) Regulations 2010.[4]

---

3   The 2002 regulations for England are available at www.opsi.gov.uk/si/ si2002/20020057.htm, 2008 at www.opsi.gov.uk/si/si2008/uksi_20080240_ en_1 and 2009 at www.opsi.gov.uk/si/si2009/uksi_20090394_en_1, all accessed on 4 July 2010. The Welsh regulations are available at www.opsi.gov.uk/ legislation/wales/wsi2003/20030327e.htm, accessed on 4 July 2010.

4   Expected to be brought into force on 1 April 2011.

The Department Education (DfE)[5] in England and the National Assembly in Wales also set National Minimum Standards for fostering.[6] These are not mandatory like Acts or Regulations but they are authoritative guidance on good practice. Agencies are inspected against these standards and falling short could ultimately result in a private agency having its registration cancelled.

Carers' registration

Currently there is no national registration scheme for foster carers, unlike other members of the children's workforce. This is likely to change, reflecting the increasing professionalism of fostering. Currently carers are assessed and approved by individual fostering agencies.

Fostering agencies

A fostering agency is either:

- a local authority fostering service, or

- a private or voluntary organisation providing fostering services to local authorities, usually known as an independent fostering agency (IFA).[7]

Agencies recruit, assess, support, train and supervise their own carers. IFAs often provide a specialist service and can appear more expensive for the local authority than placements from their own resources.

Placement with IFA carers

Leo is in the care of Borsetshire Council. He has a significant disability and Borsetshire cannot find suitable foster carers of its own. It asks Supercarers, a registered IFA, if it can provide a suitable

---

5   The Department for Education replaced the Department for Children, Schools and Families in May 2010.

6   English National Minimum Standards for Fostering, first issued in 2002, are under review at the time of writing. Welsh National Minimum Standards for Fostering Services. Available at www.csiw.wales.gov.uk/docs/Standards_Fostering_e.pdf, accessed on 4 July 2010.

7   Care Standards Act 2000 s4(4). Available at www.opsi.gov.uk/acts/acts2000/ukpga_20000014_en_1, accessed on 4 July 2010.

foster placement. Supercarers suggests Megan and Nigel who are approved as carers for children with disabilities. Borsetshire must by law satisfy itself that this is the most suitable placement for Leo in the circumstances. Having found out more about the couple, it agrees that it is a good match, so Leo is placed with Megan and Nigel, who live in the next-door county, Camfordshire.

Borsetshire is the 'responsible authority' for Leo. It must arrange and pay for his accommodation and maintenance, and safeguard his welfare. It holds PR (shared with Leo's parents) because of the care order,[8] and it employs Leo's social worker.

Supercarers arranges and supports the placement. A detailed contract between Borsetshire and Supercarers sets out exactly how tasks are shared between them. Supercarers employs Megan and Nigel's fostering social worker (sometimes called a 'support' or 'link' worker).

Megan and Nigel are responsible for Leo's day-to-day care but do not have PR for him. Their responsibilities are set out in a detailed foster placement agreement.

Camfordshire is the 'area authority' (sometimes called a 'host authority'), where the carers actually live. It was notified when the couple were approved as foster carers and now must be notified of Leo's placement because it may have to provide services such as education.

Registering and inspecting fostering agencies

Fostering agencies must be registered under the Care Standards Act 2000. Ofsted in England and the Care and Social Services Inspectorate in Wales (CSSIW) register IFAs and inspect all fostering agencies, including local authority fostering services. Inspections must be carried out at least once every three years.

Legal requirements for fostering agencies

There are complex and detailed requirements set out in the legally binding Regulations and amplified by the authoritative guidance of the National Minimum Standards.

---

8   For more information about care orders, see Chapter 6.

RESPONSIBLE PERSON AND MANAGER

A named individual must be registered as 'carrying on' an IFA and a different person appointed as the agency's registered manager. Local authority fostering services must appoint a named manager. These must be people of integrity, fit to run a fostering agency, who act with care, competence and skill.

STAFF

Agencies must have sufficient suitably qualified, competent and experienced staff. What is a 'sufficient' number depends on the size of the organisation, the number of children placed, their needs and the agency's purpose, bearing in mind the duty to safeguard and promote fostered children's health and welfare at all times.

Staff must all be 'fit' people who receive appropriate training, supervision and appraisal. The agency must keep an up-to-date record of all staff.

STATEMENT OF PURPOSE

Every fostering agency must produce:

- a statement of purpose setting out its aims, objectives, facilities and services, and which must be put into action

- a children's guide summarising in an appropriate way key information about the agency (including how to obtain an independent advocate and how to complain); different versions may be needed for different groups of children.

Agency duties

All fostering agencies have to comply with their statutory duties including:

SAFEGUARDING AND PROMOTING CHILDREN'S WELFARE AT ALL TIMES

Agencies must promote a child's:

- contact with parents, relatives and friends (subject to any court orders or contact agreements and always subject to the child's welfare)

- health and development
- educational attainment
- leisure interests.

FACTORS TO CONSIDER

Before making any decisions affecting a child who is or may be fostered, agencies must give due consideration to the child's:

- wishes and feelings (taking age and understanding into account)
- religious persuasion
- racial origin
- cultural and linguistic background.

POLICIES AND PROCEDURES

Agencies must produce policies and procedures covering:

- allegations of abuse or neglect
- acceptable measures of control, restraint and discipline, which must not include corporal punishment. Restraint must only be used where necessary to prevent injury to a child or others, or serious damage to property, and measures to control a fostered child must never be unreasonable or excessive
- children who go missing from their foster homes, including searches to be made, who is to be notified, when and how, and procedures when the child is found
- complaints by children or foster carers.

Well-run agencies provide foster carers with a handbook containing all the agency's procedures.

CARING FOR CARERS

Agencies must give carers the training, advice, information and support (including out of hours) necessary in the interests of their fostered children.[9]

---

9   For more information on training and support, see Chapter 4.

KEEPING RECORDS

These include:

- a register of fostered children

- a register of foster carers

- a case record for each approved foster carer

- a record of all unsuccessful applicants to become foster carers

- a record of any accidents involving fostered children.

Records must be kept securely. As well as the Regulations, agencies must comply with the Data Protection Act (DPA) 1998. This governs how personal data must be kept, including secure storage, and how the information may be used – fairly, lawfully and only for the purpose for which it was provided. It also gives you the right to see information stored about you and to correct any inaccuracies. Like all organisations registered under the DPA, fostering agencies can be inspected by the Information Commissioner, who can also consider complaints and has the power to prosecute.[10]

Points for practice

Make sure you:

- know who is responsible for your fostering agency, including the name of the registered manager

- have a current copy of your agency's statement of purpose and children's guide(s)

- have an up-to-date copy of all your agency's policies and procedures.

---

10   For more information about the DPA, see the Information Commissioner's helpful website at www.ico.gov.uk.

Chapter 2

Becoming a Foster Carer

Recruitment, assessment and approval

A fostering agency must assess anyone who wants to be a foster carer and may be suitable. Agencies must also keep an overview of their approved carers to see what resources they are offering. This is especially important for local authorities who must try to provide carers appropriate for the children they look after, particularly considering diversity issues. Recruitment drives may be needed to attract carers from particular backgrounds.

There are very few limits on who can foster, subject to a favourable assessment: there is no upper age limit (many people come to fostering after raising their own families); carers do not have to be homeowners and they may be single, married, divorced, in a civil partnership or cohabiting; they may be gay, straight, bisexual and of any race, cultural or linguistic background (although functional English is indispensable); and they may belong to any religion or none. There are only two statutory prohibitions: certain criminal convictions and 'barring' by the Independent Safeguarding Authority (ISA).

Automatic bar to fostering

People who have been convicted as adults of certain offences are not eligible to be foster carers, no matter how old the conviction, how completely reformed the person is and how wonderful they are in every other respect. This is an absolute prohibition and there is no appeal.

These convictions are listed in the Regulations,[1] and include assaulting a child causing injury, sexual offences against children and possessing child pornography.

Vetting and barring scheme[2]

Fostering is a 'regulated activity' under the vetting and barring scheme administered by the ISA, so a fostering agency cannot take anyone on as a foster carer without first ensuring that the person is not 'barred'. A criminal offence is committed both by the individual and the agency if a barred person works as a foster carer.

The Safeguarding Vulnerable Groups Act 2006 also proposed a registration system for everyone working with children and vulnerable adults, with carers receiving an individual number which would stay with them permanently. Agencies would be able to check that prospective carers were ISA registered. The scheme was due to commence from July 2010 but the government elected in May 2010 decided to 'review the criminal records and vetting and barring regime and scale it back to common sense levels', so at the time of writing the scheme is on hold. Check with your agency or Fostering Network for up-to-date information.

Even if the ISA registration scheme is implemented, it will not rule out the need for assessment and CRB checks to be carried out; convictions or concerns that do not lead to automatic barring are still relevant considerations in a fostering assessment.

Information about potential carers

An agency must obtain full details about potential carers, listed in Schedule 3 to the Regulations.

Assessment

Oliver and Penny apply to Supercarers to become foster carers. Their worker, Quentin, who is assessing them, explains that he must by law obtain detailed personal information about them. Like

---

1   Regulation 27(7) in both England and Wales, although the details of the offences differ slightly.

2   Introduced by the Safeguarding Vulnerable Groups Act 2006. This single scheme for people working with children or vulnerable adults replaces the previous Protection of Children Act List, Protection of Vulnerable Adults List and List 99.

most agencies, Supercarers use the 'Form F' assessment to structure its report.[3] The information covers the following areas:

- Oliver's and Penny's full names, address, dates of birth.

- Full details of the other adult in their household – the couple's 19-year-old son Robert, who spends holidays from university at home.

- Full details of their children, whether or not they still live at home, and any other children in the household – the couple's 23-year-old daughter Sarah, who now lives in her own flat, and their 17-year-old niece Tamsin, who has lived with them since her mother died three years ago.

- Their marriage and previous relationships. They married in their mid-20s and the marriage has been stable and happy, with the usual ups and downs. Neither has been married before. Quentin explains that people who have been through divorce or other relationship difficulties can be approved as foster carers: the key is to find out what went wrong and what people have learned through their experience, and to assess the strength of the current relationship, knowing the strains that fostering can place on a family.

- Their personalities. Quentin assesses this over time, carrying out interviews with each of the couple individually as well as seeing them together and taking up references. He goes over their life stories and experiences, and forms an assessment of them both.

- Their accommodation. Is it warm, comfortable and clean, big enough for a child to have his own space? Are there enough bedrooms (sharing bedrooms is a particularly sensitive issue)? Is it reasonably safe and child-friendly? Is there a safe garden? Is it suitable for a child with disabilities?

- Their racial origin, religion, cultural and linguistic background. They are white British, university-educated professional people. They are worried that their 'conventional' background might be held against them. This is not the case: it is simply part of the assessment to find out who they are, their experiences and attitudes, and whether they can care for the sort of children the agency might place, possibly including a child from a different background to their own.

---

3   Produced by British Association for Adoption and Fostering (BAAF). For more information, see their website at www.baaf.org.uk.

- They are practising Catholics and their faith is part of their motivation for wanting to foster. Quentin explores with them whether and how they could cope with a child from another faith or none, or one who is antagonistic towards their religion.

- The couple's employment, past and present, their standard of living, and their leisure activities and interests. Quentin explains that there is no 'right' answer to any of the questions: all the information is gathered to give a full picture of the couple and their lifestyle.

- Previous experience of caring for children, their own and others, and their skills, competence and potential to care for any future foster child. Quentin goes into detail about their parenting experience. Far from wanting them to be perfect parents who sailed through with no difficulties, he is keen to know about the problems they faced with their own children, how they coped and what they learned. He is also interested in how they coped with bringing Tamsin into their family. Although this is not the same as fostering an unrelated child, it gives Quentin a valuable insight into how the couple absorbed into their family a young person who arrived in difficult circumstances. He also talks to Tamsin in detail to hear her perspective. He is interested, too, in the couple's activities with children outside the family – Oliver's experience coaching rugby juniors and Penny's role with the Brownies.

- The outcome of any previous applications to foster, adopt, child-mind or otherwise look after children. A previous rejection would not mean automatic rejection of this application – circumstances might be very different – but it would obviously require detailed investigation.

Oliver, Penny, Robert and Tamsin each have to have an enhanced CRB check, including a check of the ISA barred list.

Potential foster carers must declare any convictions and cautions, even 'spent' convictions that do not normally have to be declared on job applications. Oliver's certificate confirms what he already disclosed – a caution for being drunk and disorderly when he was 20. He is deeply ashamed that this still appears on his record, but Quentin reassures him that most convictions are just another factor for consideration in the assessment.

Enhanced checks also include 'soft' information about concerns that did not result in a criminal record but are relevant to caring for children. An example of this was considered by the Supreme Court, which decided that the police were right to disclose to a school that a prospective playground assistant (who had no convictions) had been accused of neglecting her own children and not co-operating with social workers.[4]

No-one other than the prospective carers and people in the agency directly concerned with their recruitment ever sees the information on a CRB certificate. It would be a criminal offence for Supercarers to tell anyone else (such as a parent of a fostered child) about Oliver's caution.[5]

Oliver and Penny must give the names of at least two referees to provide personal references for each of them. These should be people who really know them well, in order to give a 'warts and all' picture. A written reference is not sufficient: Quentin must interview the referees and write a report. Oliver and Penny will not see this part of Quentin's report: referees must feel able to speak frankly.

The couple must each have a medical. The doctor compiles a report on their health, any medical conditions, medication and any relevant family history: the agency needs to know whether the couple will be physically and mentally fit to look after a fostered child. Fortunately, neither smoke – Supercarers has a very strict policy about smokers as carers.

As Supercarers is an IFA, Quentin must also contact the local authority where the couple live to find out its views.

Pre-approval training

As well as being assessed, prospective foster carers undergo a programme of training.[6] If a couple propose to care jointly, both must take part. In England guidance issued by The Children's Workforce Development Council recommends that pre-approval training should be completed within six months of application to become a foster carer.[7] It should give

---

4   *R (on the application of L) (FC) (Appellant) v Commissioner of Police of the Metropolis* [2009] UKSC 3.
5   s124 Police Act 1997, available at www.opsi.gov.uk/acts/acts1997/ukpga_ 19970050_en_1, accessed on 4 July 2010. Criminal Records Bureau Code of Practice, available at www.crb.homeoffice.gov.uk, accessed on 4 July 2010.
6   Many agencies use the 'Skills to Foster' programme developed by the Fostering Network.
7   Guidance available at www.cwdcouncil.org.uk/assets/.0000/0588/FC_Guidance_ for_Managers_Supervising_Social_Workers_Train.pdf, accessed on 7 July 2010. At the time of writing, the Welsh Assembly government is working with the Care Council for Wales to develop a Foster Care Training, Support, Development Induction Standards Framework.

prospective carers a realistic picture of what fostering involves, including input from experienced carers. It should cover anti-discriminatory practice, the implications of fostering for the carer's own family, and the agency's aims, policies and procedures.

Assessment

Obtaining information and providing pre-induction training is just the start. The agency's duty is to assess potential carers, so all the information about them must be analysed and a view reached as to whether they are suitable to become foster carers. Each agency has its own policies and expectations beyond the strict legal requirements.

In our example, Quentin prepares a full report on his assessment of Oliver and Penny, setting out all the information and applying his social work skills to analyse their strengths and weaknesses as potential foster carers. He must be fair to Oliver and Penny but his primary concern is to consider the children who might one day be placed with them.

The application then goes to a fostering panel.

Fostering panels

All fostering agencies must by law have at least one fostering panel, which may be established jointly with other agencies. The panel:

- considers all applications for approval as foster carers – nobody can be approved without being considered by a panel

- recommends whether an applicant is suitable to become a foster carer (this recommendation must be taken into account when a decision is made)

- recommends the terms of approval (e.g. a specified number of children within a specified age range)

- recommends whether approval should continue, and on what terms, at each carer's first annual review (and at any other time if asked)

- considers any written representations challenging

  o a refusal to approve someone as a carer

- ○ a decision to terminate approval

- ○ a change in the terms of approval

- advises the agency on its review procedures

- oversees how assessments are conducted

- gives advice and make recommendations on any issue if asked by the agency.

Fostering panel membership

Panels bring together people with relevant expertise and responsibility. There are no more than ten people on a panel and all are police-checked. They must include the following:

- A panel Chair – a senior member of staff (who does not manage the staff who conduct assessments) or an independent person with the necessary skills and experience.

- A Vice-Chair who takes over in the absence of the Chair.

- At least two social workers employed by the agency, one with child care expertise and the other with fostering service expertise, ensuring professional social work input to the panel.

- The registered provider (for an IFA) or at least one elected councillor (for a local authority) ensuring that someone with high-level responsibility for the agency is directly involved in approving its carers.

- At least four other people to provide an independent voice – they must not be agency employees, foster carers, managers (or, for a local authority, councillors) or related to an employee or manager. At least one independent member must be a current or recent foster carer from a different agency, ensuring a practical, realistic and objective viewpoint. It is good practice, but not a legal obligation, for one independent member to have personal experience of being fostered as a child or of being the parent of a fostered child.

Panel members are appointed for up to three years at a time and cannot serve for more than three terms, although they can re-join the panel after a gap of three years. They can resign at any time on a month's written notice, and can be dismissed on written notice from the agency.

Panel meetings

Panel meetings cannot go ahead unless five panel members are present, including at least the Chair or Vice-Chair, one social worker and two independent members. Agencies must have written policies and procedures about how the panel functions, including what happens if there is a split decision.

Panels consider the reports prepared by the agency. They can ask for more information or assistance from the agency if need be, and they can also seek medical or legal advice.[8]

There is as yet no legal requirement to invite applicants to the panel meeting considering their application, although it is increasingly accepted as good practice to do so.

Detailed minutes must be kept of all meetings, panel recommendations and the reasons behind them.

Going to a panel meeting

Quentin completes his assessment of Oliver and Penny and compiles a thorough report, which he goes through with them (except the information from his interviews with the referees, which remains confidential). Oliver is unhappy with the wording of one paragraph. Quentin explains that he will not change it because it is factually accurate and reflects his assessment, but Oliver's written comments will be added to the panel papers.

After months of intensive assessment, Oliver and Penny have an anxious wait before the panel day. They take up the opportunity to attend part of the panel meeting. The panel Chair comes out to introduce herself and to explain the procedure of the meeting before they go into the room. The panel members all introduce themselves and then ask a few questions. The couple are asked if they have anything they want to say, so they simply try to explain

---

8   Inserted by the Fostering Services (Amendment) Regulations 2009 in England and the Fostering Services (Amendment) (Wales) Regulations 2010.

why they want to foster. They and Quentin are asked to leave while the panel completes its deliberations.

The panel cannot tell them the outcome on the day because it only makes recommendations, not decisions, so a short but anxious wait follows.

Agency decisions

A fostering panel does not make the decision on approval or otherwise: it only makes a recommendation. The decision is made by the agency. No panel members are involved in the decision – the whole idea is that it is a two-stage process. The agency decision maker must take the panel's recommendation into account, but does not have to follow it – this is not just a rubber stamp.

Approval notice

If someone is approved as a carer, the agency must give a written notice of the approval and its terms, such as the number, age range or category of children the carer is approved to take. Sometimes this is very specific, perhaps for a named child only (e.g. when a local authority approves a friend or family member to care for a particular child), or it can be for a defined category of children such as adolescents or children with disabilities.

Carers cannot usually be approved for more than three unrelated children because CA89, Schedule 7, sets this as the 'usual fostering limit' so that foster care does not become institutional. An exception is made if the children are all siblings, because they should be placed together if this is both possible and consistent with their welfare. Carers can also seek an exemption from this limit, which can only be granted by the area authority (that is, the local authority where the carer lives) – not the fostering agency or the placing authority.

Foster care agreement

The newly approved carer and agency must enter into a foster care agreement. Regulations specify what must be included.

Approval

The panel recommends Oliver and Penny for approval as foster carers for up to two children aged from 5 to 18. The following day, Ursula, Practice Director of Supercarers and a qualified social worker herself, considers all the reports about the couple and the minutes of the panel meeting. She makes sure that all relevant matters have been covered and that she is satisfied with the quality of the assessment. She considers the panel's recommendation and decides that it is the right one. She makes the decision on behalf of the agency to approve Oliver and Penny as foster carers.

Oliver and Penny are notified in writing of their approval.

Foster care agreement

Quentin delivers the approval notice by hand and goes through with the couple the foster care agreement, which Regulations require them to enter into with Supercarers. In the agreement Supercarers sets out:

- the terms of their approval

- the support and training the couple will receive

- the procedure for review of their approval (at least annually, including an annual inspection of the home)

- procedures for placing children and an outline of what will be included in a foster placement agreement or placement plan when a child is placed

- arrangements for ensuring that any legal liabilities Oliver and Penny incur as a result of a placement are met by Supercarers (or its insurers)

- procedures for the couple to make any representations or complaints.

Oliver and Penny must agree to:

- notify Supercarers in writing of any relevant change in their circumstances

- not use corporal punishment (this is a legal requirement – agencies have no discretion)

- keep confidential any information about a child or her family and not to disclose it without the placing authority's consent

- comply with any foster placement agreement when a child is placed
- care for fostered children as if they were their own and promote their welfare
- comply with Supercarers' policies and procedures
- co-operate with inspections
- keep Supercarers informed about any fostered child's progress and inform the agency immediately of any significant events
- allow a placed child to be removed if the placement is no longer suitable.

Case record

As soon as the couple are approved, Supercarers need to set up a case record for them, which must be kept, securely and confidentially, for at least ten years after they finish fostering for the agency. This includes:

- assessment information
- report(s) to the panel
- the panel's recommendations
- the notice of approval and any later amendment
- the foster care agreement.

In due course it will also include:

- information obtained for and reports of reviews of the couple's approval
- a record of every child placed with the couple giving the child's name, age and sex, the dates of the beginning and end of the placement, plus reasons for the placement ending
- information obtained when the couple's approval finally comes to an end.

Supercarers, also enters the couple's details on their Register of Foster Carers, which records the following information for each of them:

- name, address, date of birth and sex

- dates of approval and each review
- current terms of approval.

Induction training

As soon as the couple are approved, their fostering officer gives them a copy of Supercarers' Fostering Handbook and arranges induction training to ensure that they are fully familiar with the organisation, what is expected of them and where to go for more information or help.

As Oliver and Penny are in England, they are expected to complete the Training, Support and Development Standards (developed by the Children's Workforce Development Council) within their first year as approved carers. Within six weeks of approval, their fostering officer meets them to draw up their personal development plans identifying their training and support needs.[9]

Unsuccessful applications

In practice, when it becomes clear that applicants are unsuitable, the fostering officer works with them to understand why recommendation is unlikely and they often pull out before the process is complete. However, if the application does proceed, the panel considers the case in the usual way. It makes its recommendation and gives reasons, which are then considered by the agency decision maker. The decision maker is not bound to accept the panel's recommendation and could approve the applicant in spite of the panel's contrary view. However, if the decision maker agrees, the applicants are notified of the proposal not to approve them and the reasons why. They then have 28 days to make representations or to seek an independent review. A final decision is not made until the 28 days are up, or until the conclusion of any representations or review process.

Unsuccessful applicants

Victor and William apply to Supercarers to become foster carers. Quentin carries out a full assessment and explains to the couple that he is unlikely to recommend them and why. He suggests that they consider withdrawing, but they insist on proceeding. Quentin completes his assessment and concludes, sadly, that despite the

---

9   For more information on training and support, see Chapter 4.

couple's many strengths he cannot recommend approval for the following reasons:

(a) Victor has had a number of short-lived relationships and a pattern of leaving as soon as difficulties arise.

(b) The couple's relationship is relatively new and untested. Quentin is not confident that it would stand the strain of fostering.

(c) William has experienced periods of depression and Quentin's assessment is that he is vulnerable.

(d) The couple have no experience of parenting and limited involvement with children, despite Quentin's advice to them during the assessment process to gain more experience.

The panel considers all the reports and hears from the couple themselves. It recommends that they should not be approved as foster carers and adopts Quentin's reasons as its own.

Ursula then considers the case as the agency's decision maker. She looks at the papers particularly carefully, conscious that she must not simply rubber stamp the panel's view. She concludes that Quentin has carried out a thorough assessment and she proposes to agree with the panel's recommendation. However, she does not yet make a final decision because first Victor and William must be given notice of the proposal not to approve them, with reasons and an explanation of the three choices they now have. They can:

1. accept the decision (they can confirm this in writing or do nothing, when the decision will become final in 28 days)

2. submit written representations to Supercarers within 28 days. If they do this, the panel is re-convened to reconsider the case including the couple's representations

3. apply within 28 days for review under the Independent Review Mechanism (IRM).[10]

Victor and William do not accept the decision and cannot see the point in asking the same panel that has already rejected them to look

---

10   Available from 1 April 2009 in England and 1 April 2010 in Wales; introduced by the Independent Review of Determinations (Adoption and Fostering) Regulations 2009 for England and the Independent Review of Determinations (Adoption and Fostering) (Wales) Regulations 2010.

at the case again. So they decide to opt for the IRM.[11] There is no fee for them to pay, but Supercarers have to pay a fixed contribution. They apply in writing setting out their reasons.

(a) Quentin was biased against them from the start and even tried to persuade them to give up.

(b) Quentin misunderstood Victor's previous relationships and does not recognise that this relationship is different – it is the first time that Victor has entered into a civil partnership. The couple have already withstood difficulties together.

(c) William was open and honest about his depression, which was in the past and short-lived. He is a sensitive person but that does not make him vulnerable.

(d) The decision is based on prejudice against them because they are gay. They know heterosexual foster carers who have had previous relationships and divorces but were still approved. Their lack of parenting experience is simply because as a gay couple they cannot have their own biological children together – yet they know a single foster carer who was approved in spite of being childless. The decision is based on discrimination on grounds of their sexuality and is illegal.

Under the IRM a wholly independent panel (operated by the British Association for Adoption and Fostering (BAAF) on the relevant government's behalf) looks at all the papers presented to the original panel and the couple's application to the IRM. It does not see Supercarers' panel minutes because its job is to consider the case afresh. Victor and William are invited to attend the IRM panel meeting and have up to three weeks before the panel meeting to submit any more information they would like to be considered. They receive a copy of all the paperwork the panel will consider, except confidential information provided by third parties (such as their referees' comments). Supercarers can also send up to two representatives to the IRM panel meeting.

The IRM panel holds its meeting and reaches its own recommendation with reasons. It does not overrule the original panel decision; instead it provides a separate, independent view.

Ursula now has to make the final decision for Supercarers. She

---

11   For more details as to how to apply for an IRM please see the following websites: for England www.irm-adoption.org.uk/fostering and for Wales www.irdcymru.org. uk, both accessed on 5 July 2010.

must consider the recommendation of Supercarers' own panel and also that of the IRM panel. She is not bound to accept either recommendation.

She is careful to be as objective as she can and challenges herself to ensure that she is not discriminating unfairly, knowing that it is unlawful for a fostering agency to discriminate against anyone on grounds of sexual orientation.[12] She is clear that she would make the same decision for a heterosexual couple in the same circumstances, and she knows that Supercarers has approved a number of same-sex couples as carers. She decides to accept the recommendation made by the Supercarers panel and not to approve the couple.

Supercarers notifies Victor and William of its final decision that they are not suitable for approval as foster carers together with its reasons.

Victor and William are devastated. But there is no appeal available against the agency's decision. They take legal advice but there is very little legal action available to them. They decide to wait for a while and then apply to another agency. They know that they will have to reveal their unsuccessful application to Supercarers, but they hope that another agency will consider them afresh and reach a different conclusion.

Supercarers must keep a record of all applicants who, like Victor and William, are not approved as foster carers (including those who withdraw). It must keep, securely and confidentially for at least three years, all the information gathered in the assessment, the report to the panel and the notification given to the unsuccessful applicants.

Points for practice

- Check your foster care agreement. Does it include everything it should?

- Did you receive proper induction training? If not, how could your agency's practice be improved for new applicants?

- If you are an experienced carer, consider how you could become involved in training or preparing future potential foster carers, or becoming a panel member.

---

12   Under the Equality Act Sexual Orientation Regulations 2007. Available at www.opsi.gov.uk/si/si2007/uksi_20071263_en_1, accessed on 5 July 2010.

Chapter 3

Placements

Matching

Once carers are approved, they are ready to foster a child. The next step is to match child and carer – local authorities must by law be satisfied that a particular carer is the most suitable placement for the child in the circumstances. In emergencies some compromises may have to be made.

Matching involves looking at a child's needs (including racial, ethnic, religious, cultural and linguistic needs) and the child's care plan as against the carers' characteristics and competencies, taking into account the needs of their family and any other fostered children. Location can also be an important consideration for school and contact. All relevant professionals must be involved in matching, and relevant information must be shared with potential carers to enable an appropriate decision to be made. In a planned placement, there should be a period of introductions before placement.

Matching

Megan and Nigel, foster carers approved by Supercarers, already foster Leo, who is in care to Borsetshire. They live in neighbouring Camfordshire. They are approved to foster up to two children, so they have room for another child.

Placing authority's duties

Norminster Council is accommodating Charlie,[1] who has disabilities. Only Charlie's mother Tessa has parental responsibility (PR) for him, so Norminster cannot make any decisions for Charlie without her consent.

---

1   For more information about s20 accommodation, see Chapter 6.

Norminster must first be satisfied that fostering is the most suitable way of looking after Charlie. If so, it must then find the most suitable placement for him in the circumstances. Norminster has no carers of its own who can meet Charlie's special needs, so it looks for carers from another local authority or IFA whose terms of approval are appropriate for Charlie and who have entered a foster care agreement with their agency.

Norminster contacts Supercarers. Nigel and Megan are approved carers for children with disabilities, have a place available and are interested in principle in caring for Charlie on the basis of outline information about him. If and when they are identified as a potential placement, there must be a more detailed information exchange. Norminster needs information about the couple to see if they are the most suitable placement for Charlie, and Megan and Nigel need full information about Charlie to decide whether they can indeed offer to care for him.

Norminster discusses the progress of the search for carers with Tessa, although at this stage they do not reveal identifying details. Assuming all looks promising, there are a lot of formalities to be undertaken.

Consents and notifications

The matter does not just concern Norminster, Supercarers and the couple.

Tessa must consent to the placement, or it cannot go ahead (if Charlie were subject to a care order like Leo, the local authority could proceed with a placement in the child's best interests, even against the parents' wishes). And there is another child to consider – Leo, who is already fostered by Megan and Nigel. Borsetshire is responsible for him and must be sure that his welfare will not be compromised by Charlie coming into placement – so Norminster must seek Borsetshire's consent before Charlie can be placed.

There is yet another authority involved – Camfordshire, the local authority where the couple live and which may have to provide services (particularly education but also child protection) to children fostered in its area – so Norminster must also consult Camfordshire and take its views into account, although Camfordshire cannot veto the placement.

If it decides to place Charlie with the couple, Norminster must give advance notification to:

- Tessa and Charlie's father (even though he does not have PR)

- Charlie's current carer

- Camfordshire, with a separate notification to the education department

- Charlie's existing and new GPs, health authorities and trusts.

Arrangements between the placing authority and the IFA

Arrangements must be made between Norminster and Supercarers, which are set out in detail in the Regulations. They must enter a written agreement specifying:

- the duties Norminster will delegate to Supercarers

- the services Supercarers will provide to Norminster

- how the particular foster carers will be chosen (in this case, the placement is to be with identified carers only)

- the reports Supercarers will supply to Norminster, especially following any visits supervising the placement

- how the agreement will come to an end.

There is also a more detailed agreement, specifically for Charlie's case, setting out:

- Megan's and Nigel's personal details

- the services Charlie will receive and who will provide them

- the terms of the agreement, including payment

- arrangements for record keeping, including the return of records to Norminster at the end of the placement

- confirmation that Supercarers will inform Norminster immediately of any concerns about the placement

- whether and under what circumstances other children may be placed with the couple (if Leo moved on, Norminster would have to consent before another child could be placed).

Foster placement agreement or placement plan

A detailed foster placement agreement or placement plan must be drawn up too.[2] This will cover the following:

---

2   The term 'foster placement agreement' will be replaced by the term 'placement plan' following implementation of the Care Planning, Placement and Case Review Regulations 2010 in England in April 2011.

- Charlie's personal history, religious persuasion, racial origin, and cultural and linguistic background. Megan and Nigel inevitably discover a lot of personal and sensitive information about Charlie and his family. It is a term of their foster care agreement with Supercarers that they must keep this confidential. The details the couple are given about Charlie must be a true picture including an honest assessment of any behavioural difficulties or challenges, together with Charlie's likes, dislikes, routines – indeed, anything to help them to care properly for him.

- Charlie's health, including his written health record and details of his current doctors and dentist and where he will be registered in placement. Supercarers must by law promote Charlie's health and development.

  The issue of consent to Charlie's medical or dental examination or treatment needs to be carefully thought out. Because he is not in care, only Tessa has PR. She can delegate some decisions to Megan and Nigel, perhaps including routine care so that her consent does not have to be sought each time. If Charlie sometimes needs emergency care, Tessa might authorise Megan and Nigel to take the necessary action, subject of course to her being informed urgently. The couple need to know exactly where they stand, what they can and cannot consent to, and procedures to follow when they cannot consent themselves.

  Megan and Nigel clearly need detailed information about Charlie's disability and all the implications for his care, including his safety needs and any special equipment or adaptations he requires.

- Education. Supercarers must promote Charlie's educational attainment. The agreement gives details of his current school, any proposed new school and the name of the teacher responsible for looked after children in the school. The couple also need details of Charlie's Statement of Special Educational Needs. Practical details like the respective roles of the couple and Tessa in liaising with the school, attending parents' evenings and other school functions should be spelt out to avoid difficulties later.

- Overnight stays, school trips, etc., including whether and when advance approval must be sought, and whom Megan and Nigel should contact for approval. In principle, fostered children should be able to participate in age-appropriate activities like their friends. Fostered children can feel stigmatised and frustrated if their normal activities are hampered by bureaucratic delays, and this can have a knock-on effect on their relationships with parents and carers. Everyday matters (a school day trip or a sleep-over at a friend's house) can often be delegated to the carers whereas something more significant (a school trip abroad or a holiday with a friend's family) might need advance approval. Police checks do not have to be carried out for overnight stays.[3]

Other issues also have to be considered – apparently minor things like a change of a child's hairstyle can cause great distress, so everyone needs to be as clear as possible as to which decisions the couple can and cannot make for Charlie.

- Contact. Both Norminster and Supercarers have a duty to promote contact between Charlie and his family and friends, subject to any court orders and his general welfare.

  Because Charlie is accommodated voluntarily, Tessa retains full PR and in theory could visit at any time. Depending on the circumstances, arrangements may be flexible and informal or it may be better to set out a pattern of visits and reach a shared understanding as to how arrangements are to be made.

  The couple's role in contact should be clearly set out – are they expected to have visits in their own home, transport Charlie to contact, supervise contact, help Charlie to make telephone calls, and are any special arrangements to be made for Christmas, birthdays, etc?

  Charlie's father does not have PR but he does have a contact order under s8 CA89 giving him visiting contact once a month. This order is unaffected by Charlie's accommodation in foster care and must be respected.

- Financial support for the placement, including payments for Megan and Nigel, any specific expenses arising from contact, and clear understanding as to who pays for items like school uniforms, school trips and special equipment.

- Visits and reviews. This includes arrangements for visits by Charlie's social worker and his Independent Reviewing Officer (IRO) (whose contact details must be given to the couple), and arrangements for Charlie's reviews.[4]

- Foster care agreement. Megan and Nigel must comply with their foster care agreement with Supercarers and co-operate with Norminster in any arrangements it makes for Charlie.

---

3   Local Authority Circular LAC (2004) 4 in England, Welsh Assembly Guidance November 2004 for Wales.

4   For more information about reviews, see Chapter 9.

- Ending the placement. The agreement should spell out how long the placement is expected to last and the circumstances under which Norminster might terminate it. As Charlie is accommodated voluntarily, Tessa can remove him at any time but the agreement should set out the steps to be taken should she decide to do so (even though this is not legally binding).

Placement supervision

Once Charlie is placed, Norminster must make sure that the placement continues to meet his needs. Charlie must be visited on Norminster's behalf within the first week of the placement and then at least every six weeks for the first year. After that, visits must not be more than three months apart, at any time on a reasonable request from the couple or from Charlie himself and whenever circumstances require.

On every social work visit, Charlie should be seen on his own (unless he is of sufficient age and understanding and refuses) and a report must be written up after every visit.

Support for Megan and Nigel

Supercarers must give Megan and Nigel the training, advice, information and support they need to meet Charlie's needs. They must have out-of-hours access to a fostering support worker where necessary.

Agency records

Supercarers must keep an up-to-date register of fostered children. In this must be entered:

- the date of Charlie's placement

- Megan's and Nigel's full names and address

- Charlie's address before the placement

- Norminster's details

- Charlie's legal status (accommodation under s20 CA89)

- in due course, the date the placement ends

- Charlie's address on leaving the placement.

This record has to be kept for at least 15 years after the last entry.

Ending the placement

The nature and likely duration of the placement should be clear at the outset. Some placements are always intended to be time-limited; others are indefinite, subject to continual review. If at any time the placement is no longer the most suitable way of meeting the child's needs, the placing authority must make alternative arrangements. Depending on circumstances, the child may move to another foster placement, a children's home, secure accommodation, back to a parent's care, to adoption or on to independence. Wherever possible, transitions should be made in a planned way. In an extreme case, the area authority has a duty to remove a child forthwith from a placement if it would be detrimental to the child's welfare to allow it to continue. It must immediately notify the placing authority.

Emergency placements

Sometimes children need foster care urgently. When a child has been removed from home by the police or under an Emergency Protection Order (EPO),[5] there is no time for careful matching and detailed planning: the child needs a safe place immediately. The Regulations cater for this situation by allowing an immediate placement with any approved foster carer or a temporary emergency placement with a relative or friend who is not an approved carer.

Emergency placements

Carol and David are foster carers approved by Borsetshire to provide emergency placements. They are ready to take care of a child at a moment's notice. The duty social work team calls. Three-year-old Ethan has been removed under police protection because his baby brother is in hospital with serious non-accidental injuries. Ethan needs a placement immediately. The duty social work team consider the options, as they must by law. It is unsafe to return him home until investigations have been undertaken and there are no suitable friends or family immediately available. Given Ethan's age, a children's home is inappropriate, so the duty social work team decides that fostering is the most suitable type of placement. Carol and David agree to take him. Under the Regulations, Ethan can be placed with them for up to 24 hours under a written agreement

---

5   For more information about EPOs, see Chapter 6.

specifically for use in emergencies. Under it they promise to:
- care for Ethan as if he were their own

- allow anyone authorised by Borsetshire to visit at any time

- allow Ethan to be removed by Borsetshire at any time

- keep information about Ethan and his family confidential

- allow contact with Ethan as ordered by a court or authorised by Borsetshire.

As soon as the agreement is signed, Ethan can be placed with Carol and David. A lot of work then has to be done quickly to make arrangements for when the 24 hours are up. This includes starting to look for a longer-term placement for Ethan because Carol and David only take children short term.

Points for practice
Make sure that:

- proper matching happens before a child is placed with you

- you have a comprehensive foster placement agreement or placement plan for every fostered child

- you are absolutely clear which decisions you can make for each fostered child and whom to contact for other decisions

- you are clear about contact arrangements and your role in them.

Chapter 4

Carers' Rights, Allegations and Ending Fostering

Foster carers' rights

Agencies must by law provide their carers with the training, advice, information and support they need in the interests of the children they are looking after (not in the interests of the carers themselves).

Training and development

The Regulations say that agencies must give carers the training they need. In England (work on similar provisions is in progress in Wales) the details are set out in the Training, Support and Development Standards for Foster Care.[1] Carers work through a comprehensive workbook with their supervising social worker. Agencies can use any suitable training methods to help carers achieve the Standards. The supervising social worker assesses and signs off each part of the workbook as it is achieved and, when the whole task is completed, a manager not involved in the assessment ensures that the required standards are reached. The carer then receives the Children's Workforce Development Council Certificate of Successful Completion.

All new foster carers in England are expected to complete the Standards within 12 months of their approval. Carers approved before 2008 are expected to meet the same Standards by 2011.

---

1   Accessible at www.cwdcouncil.org.uk/foster-care/standards. The Training, Support and Development Standards for Foster Care are separate from the National Minimum Standards outlined in Chapter 1.

The seven Standards are:

1. Understand the principles and values essential for fostering children and young people, including respect, confidentiality, non-judgmental approach, valuing diversity and anti-discriminatory practice.

2. Understand your role as a foster carer, including roles and relationships, legal framework, agencies' policies and procedures, relationship with parents and others, team working.

3. Understand health and safety, and healthy caring, including hygiene, first aid, personal safety and behaviour management, meeting physical, emotional, mental and sexual health needs, and giving advice on risky behaviour.

4. Know how to communicate effectively, including listening, verbal and non-verbal communication, clear jargon-free communication, communicating with parents and organisations, and keeping records.

5. Understand the development of children and young people, including attachment, developmental stages, resilience, transitions and milestones, play, activities and learning, routines, educational potential, understanding a child's social context, positive sexual health and sexual identity, supporting children with disabilities or special educational needs.

6. Safeguard children and young people, including knowledge of a child's background, and the context of legislation, policies and procedures. It also involves understanding types of abuse and neglect, signs, indicators and action to take, inter-agency working and whistle-blowing.

7. Develop yourself, including understanding the foster carer's role, its impact on the wider family, using support and supervision, and continuing to develop skills and knowledge.

Foster carers may have additional training needs such as English language skills, literacy, numeracy or computer skills. These should also be part of their training programme.

Information
INFORMATION ABOUT THE AGENCY

Carers need to have a good understanding of their own agency. Agencies should give all carers a comprehensive handbook containing:

- all policies and procedures

- guidance

- legal information

- insurance details

- the statement of purpose with details of the management structure and the agency's services, aims, objectives and principles

- copies of the children's guide[2] (possibly several versions for different groups of children).

INFORMATION ABOUT FOSTERED CHILDREN

As a carer, you are entitled to all the information you need to do your job properly, and you must feel empowered to insist on receiving it. Both the placing authority and your agency have legal duties to ensure you have all the information needed to care for the child appropriately.

Carers must be given an honest, full picture of the child and his history, including complications and difficulties, and why any previous placement broke down. A fear that a placement might not be found for a child if the truth is known is not a good reason to withhold that information. Similarly, confidentiality or the fact that the information is embarrassing for the young person is not a reason to withhold information essential to meet his needs. Instead, the child should be helped to understand what information must be shared and why, while being reassured that carers know and understand their duties of confidentiality.

Ministers have highlighted the importance of carers receiving proper information so they can decide whether to take on a particular child, can

---

2   See p.22 for more information on children's guides.

meet children's needs and can ensure the safety of fostered children and others.[3]

The Essex County Council case[4] is a cautionary tale for everyone involved in fostering. The Ws were foster carers specialising in caring for adolescents. As they had four children of their own aged between 8 and 12, they were absolutely explicit that they could not accept a placement of a young person who was a known or suspected sexual abuser. Both their agency and the social worker knew this. Despite that, a 15-year-old was placed with them. His file showed, and the social worker knew, that he had admitted sexually abusing his sister and was under investigation for rape. The inevitable happened. During a month in placement, he seriously sexually abused the Ws' children causing physical injury to them and psychological damage to both them and their parents. The case went to the House of Lords, which gave the family the right to sue Essex for negligence.

The Essex case was an extreme case, but less dramatic examples still affect the quality of care children receive and carers' ability to do their job.

THE DATA PROTECTION ACT (DPA)

Withholding information sometimes seems to be a result of paranoia about the DPA. People often wrongly think that it forbids sharing of information. In fact it is not a barrier to sharing information: instead it provides a framework for doing so properly. None of us would want our sensitive personal information given out freely, so the DPA makes it clear that information cannot be disclosed without good reason, and that it must only be used for the specified purpose and not for any other reason. Legitimate reasons for disclosure include the performance of statutory duties – such as the local authority's statutory duty towards

---

3   In England, Children's Minister Delyth Morgan's letter of 24 September 2009. Available at www.dcsf.gov.uk/everychildmatters/publications/documents/laeconsultationonnationalminimumstandards, accessed on 5 July 2010. In Wales, Deputy Minister for Social Services Gwenda Thomas's letter of 14 December 2009. Available at www.fostering.net/news/2009/wag-clarifies-rules-information-sharing, accessed on 5 July 2010.

4   *W 1-6 (AP) v Essex County Council and another* [2000] House of Lords. Available at www.publications.parliament.uk/pa/ld199900/ldjudgment/jd000316/w1-6.htm, accessed on 5 July 2010.

its looked after children, and its duty under the Regulations to disclose the information carers need in order to look after their fostered child.

CONFIDENTIALITY

It is vitally important for foster carers to understand the need to respect confidentiality; they are certainly not entitled to chat to their friends about all the fascinating details of a child's life. The information they are given must not go any further unless it is for the child's sake, and even then it is often best if the child's social worker, not the carer, discloses the information.

INFORMATION ABOUT CARERS

Of course information sharing goes both ways. A placing authority needs information about potential carers to find a suitable match for a child. This involves disclosing some sensitive personal information about carers, so the principles in the DPA apply, and local authorities receiving the information must maintain their confidentiality. Your agency should clearly explain what information about you they will share with whom, why, when, how and subject to what conditions.

Support

By law, your agency must provide you with support, including during out-of-office hours. The Standards say that you should receive supervision from a named qualified social worker who should meet you regularly and carry out at least one unannounced visit a year. Support may also include respite, peer support, independent support (especially in case of conflict, dispute or allegations), membership of foster care associations, support for your own children and support for particular groups of carers such as those from ethnic minorities or male carers.

Payment

Foster carers should receive an allowance covering the full cost of caring for each fostered child. In England, the government annually publishes recommended minimum allowance figures for different age groups and different geographical areas. These minimum figures are just to ensure that carers are not left out of pocket – agencies may of course pay more.

In Wales there is no recommended minimum allowance at the time of writing.

With ever greater professionalism demanded of them, it is becoming increasingly common for foster carers to receive a professional fee on top of the allowance, but this is not a statutory entitlement. Fees vary between agencies and may differ according to the complexity of the fostering task and the carer's expertise; however, they are usually only paid when a child is in placement and even the most generous payments do not equate to the minimum wage given the number of hours worked. Foster carers are self-employed for tax purposes.

Reviews

All foster carers must have their approval reviewed at least annually. The first annual review must be considered by the panel, and other reviews may be. As part of the review, the agency must carry out any enquiries necessary to ensure that the carers and their household remain suitable. This includes seeking the views of:

- the carers themselves

- any child placed with them over the past year (subject to the child's age and understanding)

- any local authority that has had a child in placement over the past year.

The agency must then prepare a report discussing whether the carer and the household remain suitable, and whether the terms of the approval continue to be appropriate. The carers are notified in writing of the decision, which may be to:

- continue approval on the same terms

- change the terms of approval (giving reasons for the change)

- terminate approval.

If the agency proposes to alter or terminate approval, the carers have the same rights to make representations or seek review as unsuccessful applicants for approval.[5]

---

5   As described on p.36.

A copy of the decision notice is kept on the carers' case record and their entry on the Register of Foster Carers is updated.

Complaints and allegations

Fostering is inherently vulnerable: much of the 24-hour-a-day job that is fostering takes place behind closed doors with no independent witnesses. Both foster carers and fostered children are vulnerable. A child away from home, who has already been abused or neglected, is an obvious target for those with evil intent. Foster carers may be under considerable stress coping with extreme behaviours in their own homes; some may crack under the strain and behave in an uncharacteristic way. Children who are already damaged may become aggrieved and make formal complaints about what may seem to be trivial matters; or, for whatever complex psychological reason, they may make serious allegations that are, in fact, untrue. Parents of fostered children may make allegations that are malicious, based on a misunderstanding or well-founded, motivated by anger, jealousy or love and concern for their child.

It is a sad fact that many foster carers will at some time in their fostering career face some form of complaint about their practice, or an allegation of abuse or neglect. Agencies must of course take all complaints and allegations very seriously: some are genuine.

Who is involved?

Agencies must by law have a policy to safeguard fostered children from abuse or neglect, and a procedure to be followed if allegations are made. Agencies involved include:

- the placing authority, responsible for the welfare of the child concerned

- the Local Authority Designated Officer (LADO) who must be informed of any allegation that any adult working with children has or may have harmed a child, committed a criminal offence against a child or behaved in a way indicating unsuitability to work with children

- the area children's services authority, responsible for any necessary child protection enquiries, which may involve the carer's own children as well as fostered children

- the police, if a criminal offence (such as assault or a sexual offence) is alleged

- the fostering agency, which must follow its written procedures and consider the implications for the foster carer's approval

- the ISA, if a carer may be unsuitable to work with children

- Ofsted in England or CSSIW in Wales, which must be informed of any serious complaint against a foster carer, the investigation and outcome of any child protection enquiry involving a fostered child.

Children in placement

One immediate issue is the protection of any children in placement when an allegation of neglect or abuse is made (by them or another child). Do they have to be moved? This is decided by the placing authority in consultation with relevant parties (including the child, the carers and the child's parents, who must be informed of the allegation in an appropriate way at an appropriate time) and after considering all the circumstances. If allegations are serious, a move is practically inevitable.

Apart from the disruption to all concerned if a child has to be moved, there are also financial consequences for the carers. During an investigation, no other children will be placed and carers are likely to lose their allowance.

In cases of serious allegations, the carers' own children could also be subject to child protection procedures.[6]

Guidance

Working Together,[7] government guidance for safeguarding children, includes guidance on handling allegations against members of the

---

6   For more information about child protection procedures, see Chapter 6.

7   *Working Together to Safeguard Children* (2010) Appendix 5. Available at http:// publications.education.gov.uk, accessed on 19 July 2010. Reference: DCFS-00305-2010.

children's workforce. Where there is no criminal prosecution, allegations that require investigation and disciplinary action should be resolved within 27 working days (10 days for the investigating officer to provide a report, 2 days for the fostering service to decide if a panel hearing is required and, if so, 15 days for the panel to meet). Unfortunately this is only guidance, not a statutory maximum.

The LADO's role is to provide advice and liaison in investigations, monitor the process and ensure it is fair, thorough and swift.

Support

The National Minimum Standards require agencies to provide independent support to foster carers undergoing an investigation. This is reinforced in the DCSF booklet *Protecting Children, Supporting Foster Carers*, as is the need to minimise delay.[8]

Clearly carers about whom an allegation is made must be told the details and given a full opportunity to respond to it. The allegation could have serious implications for their reputation and livelihood, so they have a right to a fair trial.

DCSF guidance says that carers who are being investigated should always be:

- treated fairly and honestly

- informed in writing as soon as possible about the nature of the allegation or concern

- given written information about the enquiry procedures and timescales

- provided with ongoing support by their supervising social worker

- given information about sources of independent advice and support

- informed as soon as possible about all decisions, which should be confirmed in writing.

---

8   DCSF (2009). Available at www.dcsf.gov.uk/everychildmatters/resources-and-practice/IG00082, accessed on 5 July 2010.

Allegation of abuse

David, aged nine, is in the care of Norminster and fostered by Ed and Fran who are approved by Valuecare. David's behaviour is extremely challenging. Ed and Fran are struggling. Fran has told her fostering officer that she is near the end of her tether, but no extra support has been provided. One morning, a member of staff from David's school telephones his social worker urgently. David has arrived at school with a swollen eye and fresh-looking bruises to his face. He told his teacher that his foster mother beat him up.

Procedures immediately swing into action.

Norminster, responsible for David's welfare, decides to move him straight from school to an emergency placement until longer-term plans can be made. This decision is made without telling or consulting Ed or Fran. David's mother must be informed of the circumstances and consulted about the change of plan, although Norminster may delay telling her for a short while so as not to jeopardise the child protection enquiry.

The LADO is informed and the Camfordshire duty child protection team holds an urgent strategy meeting with the police and Norminster. Enquiries begin. These are not only concerned with David – his safety is secured by his move – but also George, Ed and Fran's son. If Fran hit David, is George also at risk? Ed and Fran need advice from a specialist child care lawyer.

The police look at the case from a criminal point of view – David alleges an assault. There might be both criminal and child care proceedings, so police and social workers investigate jointly. The first Fran hears of it is when a police officer and social worker turn up on her doorstep. She is arrested and interviewed under caution at the police station. She vehemently denies hitting David although she admits shouting at him. She can only suppose that the bruising must have happened on the way to school because he often gets into fights with other boys. Fran has legal advice at the police station from a specialist criminal lawyer. She may be charged with an offence such as assault occasioning actual bodily harm.

Valuecare must conduct its own enquiry to decide whether Ed and Fran's approval as carers can continue. This involves gathering all the available evidence including Fran's response to the allegations. However, Valuecare cannot reach a conclusion until it knows the outcome of the police and children's social care enquiries. If, for example, Fran receives a caution or conviction for assaulting David causing him actual bodily harm, Valuecare's decision is a foregone conclusion because this would bar Fran from fostering. Even without a conviction, if Valuecare is not satisfied that Ed and Fran remain suitable, it must terminate their approval. While the investigation continues, no children will be placed with the couple. The sudden loss of their fostering allowance and fees, coupled with the stress of the investigation, puts the family under enormous strain.

Just at the time when they are most in need of support, Ed and Fran feel suddenly isolated. Their fostering officer is involved in the investigation, so cannot discuss the allegation with them. Valuecare allocates another social worker not involved in the investigation to support them, offering them information about the process, advice and advocacy, going to meetings with them and offering emotional support, but Ed and Fran find it difficult to confide in an unfamiliar worker. They contact Fosterline for more advice.[9]

Whatever the ultimate outcome, Valuecare should reflect on whether it needs to change its assessment procedures, or support and training for carers.

What if Ed and Fran decide to resign as carers, not waiting for the investigation to be completed? Unfortunately for them, the process does not end there. The social work and police investigations continue unaffected and even Valuecare must still reach a conclusion. This is important in case, for example, Ed and Fran later decide to apply to foster for another agency. If Valuecare determine that there is evidence Fran is not suitable to work with children, even if she is no longer their carer, it must refer her to the ISA.

Each agency must keep a careful record at every stage of the investigation. Ed and Fran would be well advised to keep careful notes too.

Ending fostering

Resigning

If foster carers decide to stop fostering, they must give written notice to the agency and the approval is terminated 28 days later. Unfortunately, the Regulations make no distinction between termination through resignation or retirement, perhaps after many years of outstanding service, and termination because of incompetence or worse.

---

9   Fosterline and Fosterline Wales are national advice services funded by the DfE and the Welsh Assembly respectively and run by the Fostering Network to provide confidential, independent and impartial advice to foster carers.

Retiring

Mary is 65. She has fostered for years, but it is finally time to enjoy her well-earned retirement. When her last fostered child moves on, she writes to Supercarers, telling the agency of her decision. Supercarers is sad to see her go, but it is entirely Mary's choice. As there are no children placed with Mary at the moment, there are no complications. Mary's retirement takes effect 28 days after the date when Supercarers receives her notice.

Resigning and changing agency

Callum fosters for Valuecare. He loves fostering but is unhappy with the agency. He decides to resign from Valuecare and to work instead for Supercarers. However, as foster carers are not centrally approved, he cannot simply transfer from one agency to another. Supercarers has to carry out its own assessment and pre-approval procedures to decide whether to approve him.

Callum gives notice to Valuecare of his intention to resign. He does not have to give any reason but in the circumstances he does so. Supercarers can start their assessment as soon as the notice is in, although it cannot approve Callum while he remains approved by Valuecare – by law, a person can only be approved by one agency at a time. The Fostering Network has devised guidelines for managing the situation when a carer wants to change agencies. Under this Transfer of Carers Protocol, Valuecare should provide Supercarers with a comprehensive written reference for Callum within 28 days.

Callum has a child, Eddie, in placement. As soon as Valuecare receives notice, it must send a copy to Camfordshire, which is responsible for Eddie. A copy must also be sent to Borsetshire, Callum's area authority.

Eddie is well settled and thriving, and Callum would like him to stay. Within 28 days of Callum giving notice, Camfordshire should convene a meeting, inviting Callum, Valuecare and Supercarers. The meeting considers how the change of agency may affect Eddie, how his plan will be followed and the arrangements between the two fostering agencies to co-ordinate de-registration by one and approval by the other. The meeting also considers Eddie's views and those of his parents.

The key decision for Camfordshire is whether continuing the placement with Callum is in Eddie's best interests. Eddie's IRO makes sure that plans for Eddie centre on his welfare, not budgetary or political considerations (for example, if Camfordshire does not normally place children with Supercarers because of its high charges). If necessary, she can take the matter right up to Chief Executive level or even to the Children and Family Courts Advisory and Support Service (CAFCASS) to consider legal action on Eddie's behalf to prevent breach of his human rights.[10]

If it is decided that Eddie should not stay with Callum, plans must be made for a move to another placement. If, however, the plan is for Eddie to stay, the objective is to achieve a smooth transition from one fostering agency to another. Considerable co-ordination is required. A timetable should be agreed (normally within three to six months) for Callum to cease fostering for Valuecare and become approved by Supercarers. Under the Protocol, Supercarers should agree to honour the placement charge paid by Camfordshire to Valuecare (even if this is lower than its normal charge) and the fees paid to Callum.

Terminating approval

An agency can terminate a carer's approval. The agency does not have to prove that carers or their household are actually unsuitable, just that it is not satisfied that they remain suitable – a subtle but important difference. The primary responsibility is to safeguard the children's welfare so it would clearly be wrong if nothing could be done without positive evidence of unsuitability. However, of course, this may feel unfair to the carers.

The procedure for terminating approval is similar to the procedure for applicants rejected as potential carers. The agency must consider any Panel recommendation before proposing to terminate approval. It must give the carer written notice of the proposal and reasons. The carer then has 28 days to accept the decision, make representations to the panel or apply to the IRM. The final decision must take into account any recommendations by the panel or the IRM. The carer is notified in writing of the decision, the date it takes effect and the reasons for it. There is no appeal from a decision to terminate approval.

---

10   For more information about potential legal action, see Chapter 9.

Points for practice

- Reflect on what training and support you need to do your job and make sure you receive it.

- Ensure you receive sufficient information about your fostered child, including family and background.

- Be conscious at all times of the principles of confidentiality and information sharing. If in doubt, ask advice.

- Make sure you have an up-to-date copy of your agency's complaints and allegations procedure. Know what to do and where to go for help if a complaint or allegation is made against you.

- Be aware of your rights to change agencies, resign or retire, and your rights if your agency seeks to change or terminate your approval. Know where to go for advice and support.

Part II
Fostered Children and Child Care Law

Chapter 5

Basics of Child Care Law

You do not have to become a legal expert to be a foster carer but it helps if you understand the fundamentals. Understanding every fostered child's legal status means you know who has decision-making responsibility. You can also help children to understand their own situations, perhaps supporting them through care proceedings.

The Children Act 1989 (CA89)

This is the most important statute dealing with the law for children and young people, including child protection.

Parental responsibility (PR)

PR is one of the key concepts underlying children's law. When it was introduced by CA89, it marked an important philosophical change – parents have responsibility for their children, not rights over them. Foster carers need to understand PR because it determines who has the power and responsibility to make decisions for children.

Who has PR?

Despite its name, PR is not always linked to parenthood or to taking responsibility. Some fathers do not have PR for their children, while some people who are not parents do have PR. Some people have PR when in fact they take no responsibility for a child; other people take responsibility but have no PR.

Mothers always have PR for their children. Age is irrelevant – even if the mother is legally a child herself and even if she is in care herself, she has PR (and may be the only person with it, unless, for example, the local authority obtains a care order over the baby).

A father has PR for his child if:

- he is married to the child's mother, or

- his name is on the child's birth certificate if the birth was registered on or after 1 December 2003 (earlier certificates do not confer PR even if the father's name is registered), or

- he and the child's mother have entered a formal PR agreement (signed, witnessed and filed at court), or

- he has obtained a PR order from the Family Proceedings Court (FPC).[1]

Step-parents married to, or in a civil partnership with, a child's parent have PR if:

- there is a formal, registered agreement with everyone who already has PR, or

- a court makes a step-parent PR order,[2] or a step-parent adoption order.

Non-parents gain PR for a child through:

- a residence order,[3] or

- a Special Guardianship Order (SGO),[4] or

- an adoption order.[5]

A local authority has PR if it has an Emergency Protection Order (EPO), Interim Care Order (ICO) or care order for that child.[6]

Foster carers never have PR for their fostered children; looking after someone else's child is the essence of fostering.

---

1   s4 CA89.
2   s14A CA89.
3   s8 CA89.
4   s14A CA89.
5   Under the Adoption and Children Act 2002.
6   For more about care orders and care proceedings, see Chapters 6 and 7 respectively.

Parents and PR

Mother
Kelly gives birth to Lily but leaves her with her own mother and disappears from her life. Even though Kelly does nothing for Lily, she automatically has PR.

Married father
Martin's marriage to Nellie lasted just long enough for Oscar to be conceived. Martin left months before Oscar was born and has never even seen him. However, because he was married to Oscar's mother, he automatically has PR.

Unmarried father
Polly and Quincy are not married but live together with their daughter who was born in 2002. Quincy's name is on the birth certificate. They are a committed couple who work together as parents. But, because they are not married and they have never entered a formal agreement or gone to court, Quincy has no PR. He is unaware of this and thinks that being a 'common-law husband' is the same as being married. In fact, there is no such thing as 'common-law marriage'.

What is PR?
PR includes all the rights, duties, powers, responsibilities and authority parents have towards children, including choosing their names and religion, feeding, maintaining, educating and looking after them. PR gives the right and responsibility to make all sorts of decisions for a child including:

- deciding on schooling
- giving or refusing permission for school trips
- consenting to or refusing medical examinations and treatment
- giving or refusing permission for holidays and activities
- signing for passports.

Clearly foster carers need to know who has PR for every child they foster.

Sharing PR

Many children have more than one person with PR. Each of these people has equal rights and responsibilities unless a court order says otherwise. Where parents are separated, the parent the child lives with has no greater PR than the other parent.

Apart from some important decisions (like changing a child's surname, leaving the country for more than a month, circumcision[7] and immunisations), any one person with PR can act alone without the others.

Someone who has an SGO has the exclusive right to make decisions without involving other people with PR.

If the local authority has a care order, PR is shared with the child's parents but not on an equal basis: the local authority has the lion's share and can overrule the parents if the child's welfare demands it.

However, local authorities do not have PR for children who are accommodated under s20 CA89, so it is vital to know whether a fostered child is in care or accommodated.

Private law court orders

What if people with equal PR disagree? That is where, if necessary, the court steps in. It can make 'private law' orders under s8 CA89 to determine disputes between individuals about:

- residence (who a child lives with)
- contact
- specific issues (the court can order something to be done), or
- prohibited steps (the court can forbid something).

The court's decision is based on the child's welfare, which is 'paramount', outweighing the adults' interests. The court can seek independent advice on the child's best interests from a social worker or CAFCASS officer by

---

7   For boys only – female circumcision is illegal.

ordering a report under s7 CA89. If the court is worried about a serious child protection issue, it can instead order the local authority to report under s37 CA89 to say whether it proposes to start care proceedings.

PR in action

Married parents

Rashid's parents are married. If he needs to go to hospital, each parent has PR and an equal right to consent to examination and treatment.

Divorced parents

Sam's parents are divorced. He lives with his mum under a residence order and has a contact order to see his dad. Apart from residence and contact (decided by the court), both have an equal right to make decisions for Sam. So if Sam needs to go to the dentist while on a contact stay, his dad can consent to treatment. But if the parents disagree about a major decision – for example, Mum wants him to go to the local comprehensive while Dad wants him to go to Eton (and is willing to pay) – the court might have to make a Specific Issue Order deciding which school Sam goes to, based on Sam's best interests.

Special guardians

Tanya lives with her Uncle Uriah and Aunt Vanessa under an SGO because of her mum Wanda's serious mental health problems. When Wanda is well, they consult her and involve her fully in decisions, but when she is ill they can make all the decisions they need to without involving Wanda at all.

Care order

Borsetshire Council has a care order for Xanthe and so has PR for her, shared with her mother Yvette. Borsetshire consults Yvette about plans, working in partnership wherever possible. Xanthe has the opportunity to go to America with the school choir, but Yvette opposes, saying that Xanthe is being spoilt. Borsetshire considers Yvette's views, but decides that the trip is in Xanthe's best interests. It overrides Yvette's opposition and gives consent.

Adopted children

Adoption is different from any other court order. It ends the birth parents' PR permanently and irrevocably. They are completely replaced by the adoptive parents who are treated in law as if they had given birth to the child, who becomes a full member of their family. The adopters become the only people with PR.[8]

Adopted child

Zachary was removed from his mother Abby. Borsetshire Council obtained a care order and a placement order, authorising his placement for adoption with Barry and Colin who apply for an adoption order. The moment the adoption order is made, PR is transferred absolutely and completely. Abby is no longer Zachary's mother and loses PR forever. The care order ends so the local authority also loses its PR. Barry and Colin are now the only people with PR for Zachary. They are legally and permanently his parents.

Delegating PR

People who have PR cannot dispose of it or resign from it. They can, however, arrange for someone else to exercise PR for them. This delegation might be limited and temporary (e.g. asking a babysitter to look after a child for the evening), or wholesale and long term (e.g. when a young teenager's baby is brought up by grandparents).

Parents who request voluntary accommodation for their child under s20 CA89 are delegating aspects of their PR to the local authority to exercise on their behalf.

Foster carers never acquire PR for fostered children in their own right, but elements of PR may be delegated to them. In general, the longer term the placement, the more decisions are delegated to the carers. As a carer, it is vital to be clear from the start which decisions you can and cannot make, and who has the authority to decide if you cannot. Failure to make this clear can lead to confusion, delay, frustration and sometimes distress for all concerned.

---

8   For more about adoption, see Chapter 17.

Emergencies

Sometimes urgent action is needed and it is neither possible nor sensible to track down someone with PR. Sometimes a person with PR is not in a fit state to make a decision. The law caters for such exceptional circumstances. For example, doctors can legally treat anyone without consent in an emergency.

For carers, s3(5) CA89 is very important. This says that someone who does not have PR but does have the actual care of the child (exactly like a foster carer) can legally do 'what is reasonable in all the circumstances of the case for the purpose of safeguarding or promoting the child's welfare'.

Medical emergency

Alice fosters Beth who starts to have convulsions. Alice does not stop to check her placement agreement to see if she has delegated authority – she just goes ahead and calls an ambulance. In fact s3(5) CA89 authorises her to do this. At the hospital, the doctors do not wait for a signed consent from someone with PR – they just start treatment. Of course, Alice contacts Beth's social worker as soon as possible to regularise the situation.

Drunken dad

Carlos fosters Duncan. Duncan's dad, Eric, arrives to take him out for contact. Eric smells strongly of alcohol, he is slurring and unsteady on his feet, yet he wants to take Duncan for a drive. Carlos thinks this is dangerous and refuses to let Duncan go with Eric. Eric shouts 'I'm his dad! You can't stop me!' Normally, he would be right – Eric has PR; Carlos does not. But does Carlos have to let Duncan get in Eric's car? In these exceptional circumstances where Duncan's safety is at risk, s3(5) CA89 authorises Carlos to refuse to let Duncan go, giving him time to contact Duncan's social worker or the police.

End of PR

PR ends:

- when a young person turns 18

- on death

- if a court revokes the order that gave the person PR in the first place

- if an adoption order is made, ending the birth parents' PR

- if a care order is revoked or replaced by another order, ending the local authority's PR.

PR is not ended by divorce or by a care order being made. PR remains even if parents decide not to exercise it. The only way a birth parent can relinquish PR altogether is by consenting to an adoption order.

Children cannot 'divorce' their parents except in very unusual and extreme circumstances. In one case, a 13-year-old girl who had been grossly abused by her father successfully applied to court to remove his PR. This was only possible because he obtained PR through a court order in the first place – if he had been married to the girl's mother, it would not have been possible. Similarly, the court cannot remove a mother's PR however appallingly she has treated her child.

In the same case, the court also authorised the local authority not to involve the father in plans for the girl's future – they only had to give him a general annual update and information about very significant life events.[9] This was only possible because the girl was in care – it would not have been an option if she had been accommodated.[10]

Young people's right to make decisions

Increasing autonomy is a normal part of development and a carer's role includes encouraging a young person to take responsibility and make decisions (including sometimes making mistakes).

---

9   *Re C (Care: Consultation with Parents Not in Child's Best Interests)* [2005] EWHC 3390; [2006] 2FLR 787, High Court.

10   For more information about care and accommodation, see Chapter 6.

Some laws set a legal age limit, which applies regardless of individual characteristics.[11] So children are criminally responsible for their actions from the age of 10, however mature or immature they are. Not even a Lewis Hamilton can get a driving licence before the age of 17 and no-one can marry under the age of 16 (even with parental consent, or 18 without it). Young people from the age of 16 can legally consent in their own right to medical, surgical or dental treatment.

But where there is no law setting a specific age, we have to consider the individual's competence. If you are in doubt about a young person's right or ability to make her own decision about a particular matter, don't risk it – take advice.

You may know the terms 'Gillick competence' or 'Fraser guidelines', coming from a case that decided that a girl under 16 with sufficient understanding could consent to contraception in her own right.[12] These principles help us judge a young person's competence to make all sorts of other decisions. Factors include the following:

- Age – simple decisions (what do you want for tea?) can be made by very young children but the more complex the decision, the older a child usually has to be to make it.

- Understanding – a child with a learning disability may be less able to take decisions a non-disabled counterpart could make.

- Emotional state – a child with no cognitive impairment may nevertheless be too traumatised to make a decision.

- Life experiences – children with long experience of medical treatment often understand more than most adults about the implications of treatment decisions.

- Information – enough age-appropriate information must be available.

- Freedom of choice – young people must be free to express their own wishes, not under pressure to 'say the right thing' or bound by misplaced loyalty.

---

11   The Children's Legal Centre produces a handy publication 'At what age can I...? A guide to age-based legislation', updated by Joanne Claridge (2008) and listing age limits for all kinds of activities.

12   *Gillick v West Norfolk and Wisbech Health Authority* [1986] AC 112.

As a carer, you probably know your fostered child better than anyone and should have important input into any assessment of her competence and capacity.

Points for practice

- Make sure you know who has PR for the children you foster, who can make which decisions for your fostered child and the extent of your own decision-making power.

- Consider what decisions your fostered child can make for himself. What useful information could you contribute to an assessment of whether your fostered child is competent to make a particular decision?

- Be aware of what s3(5) CA89 enables you to do if necessary.

Chapter 6

Looked After Children

A 'looked after' child is anyone under 18 who is cared for by the local authority. The child may be:

- accommodated under s20 CA89

- in care under a care order made under s31 CA89 (or an ICO during care proceedings), or

- remanded to local authority accommodation by a criminal court.

It is vital to know and understand the legal status of every child you foster.

Children involved in criminal proceedings are the subject of Part III of this book; the rest of Part II is concerned with children who are looked after on welfare grounds.

Accommodation

This is a purely voluntary arrangement under s20 CA89 between a child's parent(s) and the local authority. An accommodated child is not 'in care'; there is no such thing as 'voluntary care' (an outdated term still occasionally – wrongly – used). Accommodation is a supportive service to help children and families through difficulties; there is nothing compulsory about it.

Local authorities have a statutory duty to accommodate any children in need in their area who require accommodation because:

- nobody has PR for them, or

- they are lost or abandoned, or

- the people who have been caring for them can no longer do so, temporarily or permanently and for whatever reason.[1]

---

1   s20(1) CA89.

Accommodated children

Orphan

Zak's parents are both dead. There are no friends or family to look after him. Nobody has PR for Zak, so the local authority must accommodate him.

Abandoned baby

Yvonne is a new-born baby found abandoned. There is no trace of her mother. The local authority must care for her.

Temporary difficulties

Xavier's mother has to go into hospital. She has lost contact with his father and has no-one to look after Xavier while she recuperates. The local authority must make temporary arrangements for him until his mother recovers.

Respite

Will has profound disabilities. His parents look after him but need regular breaks to rest and spend time with their other children. Will needs specialist care. The local authority arranges short breaks with a foster carer with the expertise to meet his needs.

Parents who cannot cope

Vanessa is autistic and her mother cannot cope with her challenging behaviour. The local authority explores whether, with services and support, Vanessa can stay at home; if not, the local authority will accommodate her long term.

Accommodation and PR

Accommodation is a service provided by the local authority to help families, not to take over.

AGREEMENT OF EVERYONE WITH PR

The local authority can only accommodate a child if everyone with PR agrees. If in our example Xavier's father had PR and could care for

Xavier while his mother was in hospital, accommodation would not be an option. The law only allows a local authority to step in when no-one with PR is available.

THE LOCAL AUTHORITY DOES NOT ACQUIRE PR
The local authority is helping out by exercising aspects of PR (like providing accommodation and day-to-day care) on behalf of a parent, not in its own right. A proper written agreement should specify which decisions are delegated to the local authority or carer, and which must be referred back to the parent. Everything has to be agreed; the local authority has no power of its own and there can be no compulsion.

ANYONE WITH PR CAN REMOVE THE CHILD AT ANY TIME
Accommodation only lasts for so long as everyone with PR agrees. As soon as anyone with PR wants the child back, they are entitled to take him immediately. This applies even if the parent previously agreed to give notice before removing the child – that agreement is not legally binding.

Removal from accommodation

Jane admits herself voluntarily to psychiatric hospital and asks Camfordshire to find a foster carer for Kim. A written agreement is drawn up. Kim will stay in foster care for at least three months and Jane will give seven days' notice before asking to have Kim home. Kim is placed with Lorraine and settles well. Six weeks later, Jane discharges herself from hospital and asks for Kim's immediate return. The social worker asks Jane to give Lorraine a chance to prepare Kim to go home but Jane insists. The written agreement is not legally binding. Unless there are grounds for a court order to keep Kim in care, Jane's PR gives her the right to take Kim home – the local authority's job is done. This is unless Kim has turned 16 when she has the right to refuse to go.

Imagine instead it is not Jane, but Kim's father Mike who wants to take her to live with him. Mike does not have PR so has no legal right to discharge Kim from foster care. The local authority cannot allow it without Jane's clear authority. If she refuses and Mike really wants to care for Kim, he must go to court to get PR or a residence order.

The child's voice

Before a child is accommodated, the local authority must by law 'so far as is reasonably practicable and consistent with the child's welfare' find out the child's wishes and feelings and take them into account, bearing in mind the child's age and understanding. So the child must be consulted, but does not have to consent.

Children 'in care'

The other main group of children in foster care are those who are there through child protection court orders obtained by the local authority – EPOs, ICOs or full care orders.

Significant harm

All the local authority's child protection powers and duties, from initial referral through to a full care order, centre on the term 'significant harm'.

Harm means:

- ill-treatment including:
  - physical
  - emotional and/or
  - sexual abuse
- and/or the impairment of health including:
  - physical and/or
  - mental health
- and/or the impairment of:
  - physical
  - intellectual
  - emotional
  - social and/or
  - behavioural development.

This means that the term 'harm' includes all kinds of abuse and neglect.

But local authorities can only step in if the harm is 'significant'. As Ward LJ[2] explained in the Court of Appeal, harm must be 'significant enough to justify the intervention of the State and disturb the autonomy of the parents to bring up their children by themselves in the way they choose', or, as Hedley J[3] said in the High Court, it must be 'something unusual; at least more than the commonplace human failure or inadequacy'. Before a local authority can intervene, the 'significant harm' line must be crossed. This is the concept of the 'threshold criteria', a term used as shorthand for the grounds for care proceedings.

Significant harm on its own does not justify intervention: children can suffer significant harm without raising child protection issues – for example, a child who has a serious accident. So the law requires a second important element to justify making a care order – the significant harm must be due either to inadequate care or to the child being beyond parental control.

Child protection investigations

If a local authority has 'reasonable cause to suspect' that a child is suffering significant harm (or is likely to do so), it must make enquiries to decide whether any action is needed to safeguard the child. The 'reasonable cause' may come, for example, from a referral from a professional or neighbour. Other agencies have a duty to help children's social care staff with their enquiries. *Working Together* is the key government guidance that prescribes how enquiries should be conducted and how agencies are to co-operate.[4]

Child protection case conferences

These are meetings at which all the professionals (including foster carers) involved in a child's life share information to determine whether the child is at continuing risk of significant harm and should become 'subject to a child protection plan' (replacing the old Child Protection Register).

2   *Re MA, SA and HA (children, by their Children's Guardian) and MA, HA and the City and County of Swansea* [2009] EWCA Civ 853 at para 54.

3   *Re L (Care: Threshold criteria)* [2007] IFLR 2050 High Court at para 51.

4   *Working Together to Safeguard Children* (2010). Available at http://publications. education.gov.uk, accessed on 19 July 2010. Reference: DCFS-00305-2010.

Parents are normally invited to at least part of a meeting. Children who are old enough and want to attend should also do so, but even if they are not present in person their views and wishes should be reported to the meeting.

If a child is made subject to a child protection plan, a review conference is held within three months, and then every six months.

Emergency action

Sometimes there is no time to conduct a full assessment and urgent action is needed. There are two ways to protect children in an emergency: police protection or via an Emergency Protection Order (EPO). In both cases the key question is whether the children are likely to suffer significant harm if urgent action is not taken – either to move them to a safe place or to stop them being removed if they are already in a safe place.

> Rob is voluntarily accommodated in foster care with Sally. His father Ted attends the foster home for contact but becomes aggressive, grabbing Rob and threatening to take him home by force if necessary. Rob is screaming and begging not to go. Sally calls the police, who decide that Rob is at risk of significant harm and must stay in the foster home. They take Rob into police protection to stop him being removed from a safe place.

The grounds for police protection and EPOs are very similar, but the procedures are very different.

Police protection

This is an administrative action taken by the police without going to court. It lasts for a maximum of 72 hours and the police ensure that the child is moved to local authority accommodation (often foster care) as soon as possible.

EPOs

Unlike the police, social workers cannot remove children without court authority. To take emergency action, they must apply for an EPO, presenting evidence to the court to justify their application. By law, the parents should normally receive advance notice of the application, but where necessary the court can waive this and proceed without the parents even knowing about the application.

EPOs last for up to eight days, with one possible extension of a further seven days. The local authority obtains PR, shared with the parent(s) but with the local authority as 'senior partner'. This means the local authority decides where the child lives for the duration of the order, often in foster care.

Care orders

The procedures for seeking a care order are described in Chapter 7. If a child needs to be looked after by the local authority during this long process, the court can make Interim Care Orders (ICOs), placing the child in temporary care. At the end of the case, after considering all the evidence, the court can make a full care order if it finds:

- the threshold criteria are met, that is:

  o the child is suffering significant harm or is likely to do so, and

  o that harm is due to the child receiving inadequate care or to being beyond parental control

- it is in the child's best interests to make a care order (rather than another type of order or no order).

Welfare checklist

How does the court decide what is in a child's best interests? The child's welfare is paramount; the child comes first and his interests override everyone else's. The case is not about the parents and whether they are good, bad or indifferent – their lifestyle and parenting skills only matter if and so far as they affect the child. The court is not there to condemn the parents or to feel sorry for them – it is only there to decide what is best for the child. Nor is the case about the social workers and how well or badly they have done their job.

To decide on children's best interests, the court must always consider a list of factors, often known as the 'welfare checklist':

- the children's wishes and feelings, in the light of their age and understanding

- their physical, emotional and educational needs

- the likely effect on them of any change in their circumstances

- their age, sex, background and any relevant characteristics (including racial, religious, cultural and linguistic heritage, disabilities or special needs, as well as talents or abilities)

- any harm they have suffered or are at risk of suffering

- how capable their parents or other relevant people are of meeting their needs

- the court's powers.

The last factor is important because the court does not have to grant a care order just because that is what the local authority sought – it can consider all the available options including making no order at all.

> Norminster applies for a care order for Darren, planning to place him in foster care. After considering all the evidence, the judge decides that Darren should live with his grandmother Edith. He does not make the care order Norminster sought, instead giving Edith a residence order. He also makes contact orders for Darren's parents. He wants the local authority involved to 'advise, assist and befriend' Darren so he makes a supervision order for one year.

If the court is considering making a care order, it must first consider the local authority's care plan. The court cannot dictate what is in a care plan, but before entrusting a child's future to a local authority the court must know in detail what is proposed for the child.

Effect of care orders
A care order:

- gives the local authority PR with 'senior partner' status to override the parents where necessary in the child's best interests

- makes the child a 'looked after' child

- gives the local authority the duty to accommodate (possibly in foster care) and maintain the child

- lasts until the child turns 18 unless and until the court decides otherwise (by revoking the care order on an application by the parents, local authority or child, or by making another order such as an adoption order to replace the care order).

Contact with children in care

The parents of a child in care (including a father without PR) have an automatic right to 'reasonable' contact with their child. What is 'reasonable' depends on the circumstances of the case. Ideally, arrangements are made after consultation and agreement but, if this is not possible, the care order gives the local authority power to decide on contact as long as it remains 'reasonable'.

The court can dictate contact arrangements by making a contact order under s34 CA89 or by making an order under s34(4) CA89 that gives a local authority the power to refuse contact to a named person.[5]

Accommodation and care orders

Roger and Stephen are both ten years old and fostered by Mrs Timms. She treats them the same and there is no obvious difference in their day-to-day lives. Both are looked after by Borsetshire and have the same social worker. They both have regular reviews, the same IRO and Borsetshire owes them the same duties. In many ways their situations seem identical. But Roger is accommodated, while Stephen is subject to a care order.

Roger is looked after as a supportive service to help him and his family. Stephen is looked after for his protection against his parents' wishes.

Roger is looked after by agreement between his parents and Borsetshire. His parents had no legal advice, no-one went to court and Roger was not separately represented. Stephen is looked after under a court order made after the court heard everyone's evidence and arguments. Stephen, his parents and the local authority were all legally represented. The court decided the statutory grounds were met and a care order was needed.

Roger's parents have full PR for him but have delegated some decisions to Borsetshire. Stephen's parents still have PR for him, but

---

5   For more about contact, see Chapter 10.

Borsetshire also has PR and can overrule them when necessary.

Roger's parents decide how long he remains accommodated. Stephen will stay in care until he is 18 unless the court decides otherwise.

Roger's parents have contact with him on a flexible basis by agreement. Borsetshire decide Stephen's parents' contact. They try to reach agreement but, if that is not possible, Borsetshire dictate arrangements (provided they remain 'reasonable').

The dentist advises that both boys need to have a brace fitted and asks for consent. Roger's parents have delegated to Borsetshire the power to consent to routine and emergency treatment: this is neither, so the Council must ask Roger's parents for consent. If they refuse, the treatment cannot go ahead even if Borsetshire feels it should.

Borsetshire consults Stephen's parents. His mother fails to respond. His father refuses consent saying pretty teeth are not important for boys. Borsetshire considers that the treatment is in Stephen's best interests. It has PR and the power to override the parents so can consent to the treatment.

The two boys' parents have got to know each other. They agree that Mrs Timms spoils the boys and that foster care is too soft. Both couples tell the social worker that they will be removing their child from Mrs Timms and taking him home on Friday after school.

Roger's parents have exclusive PR. Unless there are grounds for a court order to stop Roger going home, his parents have every right to end the accommodation arrangement and take him home. The social worker asks Mrs Timms to pack Roger's bags and to start preparing him to leave.

Stephen is in care. Borsetshire regularly reviews whether it is safe to return him home: it is not. Because of the care order, Borsetshire decides where Stephen is placed. The social worker tells Stephen's parents that Stephen will not be allowed to return home and will remain in foster care for the foreseeable future, subject to reviews. She instructs Mrs Timms not to pack Stephen's bags, to be prepared to refuse entry to his parents and to call the police if necessary. She advises Stephen's parents to see their lawyer.

Points for practice

- Always be clear of the legal status of each child you are fostering and its implications.

- Keep in mind the legal distinctions between accommodation and care, however little difference there may be day to day.

- Ensure arrangements for delegated responsibility are clearly agreed and documented.

- Make sure you know who does and who does not have a legal right to contact with your fostered child, and be clear as to your role and responsibility regarding contact.

Chapter 7

Care Proceedings

Care proceedings

The decision to start care proceedings is one for the local authority alone, not the case conference or any other agency. Sometimes care proceedings follow emergency procedures; if a child is subject to police protection or an EPO and the problems are not quickly resolved, care proceedings may be necessary. But this is not always the case; often social workers work with a family for months, even years, before starting proceedings.

Before proceedings

The Public Law Outline (known as the 'PLO')[1] prescribes the procedure for care proceedings. Except in an emergency, the local authority must carry out a lot of work before going to court, including undertaking a core assessment. The parents should be informed in writing that proceedings are contemplated and why, then invited to a meeting along with their legal representative to discuss matters in the hope of avoiding the need to go to court, even at the last minute.

To launch proceedings, the local authority files at court:

- an application form

- a fee

- a social work chronology

- a social work statement

- a copy of the initial and core assessment

---

1   Available at www.hmcourts-service.gov.uk/cms/files/public_law_outline_PD_ April_2010.pdf, accessed on 5 July 2010.

- a copy of the letter before proceedings sent to family

- a schedule of proposed findings (setting out exactly what the local authority intends to prove to the court)

- a care plan.

Courts

Care proceedings start in the Family Proceedings Court (FPC), which is part of the Magistrates' Court. The FPC has a separate entrance and separate waiting area from the rest of the building where criminal cases are heard.

Most cases are heard by lay magistrates who are not legally qualified because their role is to represent the ordinary, commonsense lay person. They are part time and usually sit as a Bench of three with a legal adviser to help them with questions of law and procedure. In some areas you may instead come across a District Judge (Magistrates' Court) who is a professional, legally qualified magistrate who sits on his own to perform the same task as lay magistrates.

Some cases are transferred up to the County Court where they are heard by a full-time judge. Very complex cases are transferred even higher to the High Court where they are heard by a senior specialist family judge. The idea is that cases are heard in a court of the appropriate level given the length, complexity and gravity of the case.

> Chardonnay is subject to care proceedings because of alleged neglect. The local authority's case is that Chardonnay is not fed or clothed properly, the house is unhygienic, she is dirty and her medical needs are neglected. Her case is heard in the FPC. Lay magistrates are perfectly capable of judging allegations of failure in ordinary everyday care.
>
> Diana is also subject to care proceedings because of a spiral fracture to her arm. The local authority and the parents have conflicting medical evidence about the cause of the injury. Her case is more complex than Chardonnay's and is transferred up to the County Court to be dealt with by a judge.
>
> Elspeth has frequent emergency admissions to hospital. The local authority starts care proceedings because, on medical and psychiatric advice, it alleges that Elspeth's mother is deliberately poisoning her to seek attention. Elspeth's case is even more

complex than Diana's – cases of factitious or induced illness are always sensitive and difficult. The case will involve several expert witnesses and last for many days. It is transferred up to the High Court.

Parties to proceedings

The local authority brings the case: it is the 'applicant'. The other people involved are 'respondents'. They are all entitled to:

- have copies of all the documents presented to court by the local authority

- file their own evidence

- call their own witnesses

- cross-examine the local authority's witnesses, and

- be represented by a lawyer – parents and children automatically get Legal Aid for care proceedings.

The respondents are:

- the child's mother

- the child's father if he has PR (if not, he has to apply to the court to become a respondent if he wants to participate)

- anyone else with PR (e.g. someone with a residence order)

- anyone else the court decides should be a party to the proceedings

- the child himself.

If parents are not competent to instruct their own lawyers (because of mental ill-health, a learning disability or because they are under age themselves), they are represented by someone such as the Official Solicitor who conducts the case for them, ensuring that their interests are properly represented.

The child's role

The child is always a party to care proceedings in his own right because his interests may not be the same as any of the adults involved. He is separately represented by a Children's Guardian (formerly called a 'Guardian ad Litem') and a solicitor.

Children's Guardian

The court orders CAFCASS to appoint a Children's Guardian in each case. She is often referred to just as 'the Guardian' but this does not mean that she acts in loco parentis: she is only concerned with representing the child's interests in the court case. Her role starts and ends with the proceedings.

The Guardian's job is to look at the case afresh and give the court an independent expert view (Guardians are qualified social workers). She advises the court on the child's best interests, independent of the views and interests of the local authority and family members alike, and ensures that the court is clearly informed about the child's wishes and feelings. Of course, the child's wishes may not be the same as his best interests.

Guardians have enormous influence with the court.

> Georgia is 13. She is the subject of care proceedings because of her parents' drug use and domestic violence. Georgia had to fend for herself and look after her parents. She is intensely loyal to them and worries about how they will cope without her. She is adamant that she wants to return home and cannot contemplate any alternative. She behaves impeccably in her foster home in order to persuade the authorities that she has no problems and can go home. Harry, the Guardian, makes Georgia's emphatic views very clear in his report; however, having investigated the case thoroughly, his recommendation to the court is that it is in Georgia's best interests to remain in care.

The Guardian has a right to see all the statements and reports in the case and to inspect the child's social work files. She meets and talks to everyone involved in the case – social worker, parents, other professionals and family members – and may commission further evidence such as an expert report.

If the child is in foster care during the proceedings, the Guardian should visit the foster home and take time to talk in detail to the carers listening to their observations and views including any information to help the Guardian to communicate with the child. If you foster a child in care proceedings make sure the Guardian talks to you in detail.

Most importantly the Guardian should spend time with the child on his own to get to know him and to find out about his behaviour, history, needs, wishes and feelings. How often she visits will vary according to the circumstances including the child's age – obviously, she needs to meet a teenager more often than a young baby. Some meetings are likely to be at the foster home and some elsewhere. The Guardian should give the child and foster carer her contact details so that she can be contacted in case of any developments or if the child wants to talk to her.

At the time of writing, unfortunately CAFCASS is experiencing enormous pressures. Carers may need to remind CAFCASS of their own National Standard 5: 'CAFCASS will ensure that all children are seen, heard and understood and their active involvement in all aspects of their case is promoted, in a way that is consistent with and responds to each child's wishes, competence and understanding.'

Child's solicitor

As well as a Guardian, the child also has a solicitor like every other party in the case. The Guardian normally chooses the solicitor, a member of the Children Panel of specialist solicitors with proven knowledge, expertise and experience in child care law. The solicitor and Guardian work together. The Guardian carries out enquiries while the solicitor advises on law and procedure, prepares correspondence and legal documentation and represents the child in court. Unless the child is very young, the solicitor usually goes to meet him with the Guardian.

But what if the child and the Guardian disagree? The solicitor cannot advance two contradictory cases at once. Importantly, the solicitor acts for the child, not the Guardian, so if there is a disagreement and the child is competent to instruct, the solicitor represents the child against the Guardian.

> At the beginning of Georgia's case, her Children's Guardian Harry appoints Irene as Georgia's solicitor. At first Harry and Irene work together. However, it soon becomes clear that Georgia wants to go home while Harry is clear that she should stay in foster care.
>
> Irene sees Georgia on her own to talk things through. She finds that Georgia is an averagely intelligent 13-year-old who understands

what the case is about and is competent to give her own instructions. Clearly Irene cannot represent both Georgia and Harry so she tells Harry that she cannot continue to act for him and will take her instructions direct from Georgia. Harry can either represent himself in court or find another lawyer.

From this point on, Irene works with Georgia direct, going through the evidence with her, explaining the case and procedure and giving her legal advice. When the final hearing comes, Irene argues on Georgia's behalf that she should go home to her parents.

The child in court

It is extremely rare for a child to go to court to give evidence in care proceedings. In fact, it is unusual for a child to go to the family court at all, even though the case is all about the child's welfare – most judges and magistrates decide children's futures without ever meeting the children themselves. However, practice is starting to change and varies from court to court, so it is best to ask the child's solicitor or the Guardian about the approach taken in your area.

Georgia's final hearing is approaching. She is very keen to go to court to listen to the whole case and to tell the judge in person what she wants. Harry and Irene both emphasise that they will make sure the judge knows her wishes and feelings, but Georgia is not reassured. Irene applies to the judge for Georgia to be allowed to attend court for the whole hearing. The judge considers the application carefully but decides that it would not be appropriate for Georgia to hear all the evidence and the legal wrangling. However, he does agree to see Georgia at court on the first day of the hearing so she can meet him and tell him her wishes face-to-face.

The judge sees Georgia in his chambers (his private study adjoining the courtroom) together with Harry and Irene. He asks her what she wants to say, listens and makes a careful note. He tells her that he has listened carefully and takes her wishes very seriously, but he cannot make up his mind until he hears what everyone else has to say. Georgia is relieved and quite proud of herself: she has met the judge in person and has said her piece. She knows she has done what she can.

Procedure

The PLO sets out full details of procedures. Briefly the stages are as follows:

Stage 1: Issue of proceedings and first court appointment

The local authority files its application form, fee and supporting documents at court. The court issues the case, allocating a case number and sends a notice to all the respondents with a copy of the local authority's documents. It asks CAFCASS to appoint a Guardian. If the case clearly needs to be transferred up to the County Court, this is done immediately.

The first court hearing happens within six days of the application. The court gives procedural directions for the case including setting a timetable for all parties to file their statements and other evidence, and fixing future hearings, right through to a final hearing if possible.

Stage 2: Case Management Conference (CMC) (no more than 45 days after the application)

The parties' advocates must meet before this hearing to identify and narrow the issues between them and prepare a draft order. At the CMC the court checks on whether previous directions have been complied with, identifies the key issues in the case and fixes the timetable for the rest of the case.

Stage 3: Issue Resolution Hearing (IRH) (16–25 weeks after application)

Again the advocates must meet before the hearing to narrow issues. At the IRH the court again checks that previous directions have been complied with, identifies remaining issues and makes any directions necessary to ensure the final hearing goes smoothly, checking that enough court time is available, deciding which witnesses need to attend court, getting all the paperwork together and ordering the advocates to produce written arguments.

Stage 4: Final hearing (within 40 weeks of application)

The court hears oral evidence and legal submissions on the issues that remain in dispute and reaches a final conclusion.

Interim hearings and ICOs

Even assuming that the PLO timetable is met (which is not always the case), care proceedings take some nine months from beginning to end. Sometimes the child cannot be left at home while the case is going through the court. In such cases, the local authority can apply for an ICO (an interim supervision order is also possible, but that does not authorise the child's removal from home). As its name suggests, an ICO is like a care order but for a short period while proceedings continue – up to eight weeks for the first one, and up to four weeks at a time after that. ICOs give the local authority temporary PR with senior partner status, including the power to decide where the child lives, often in foster care.

If the local authority seeks an ICO and the parents oppose it, the court must hold an interim hearing to decide the issue. Interim hearings are often hotly contested because parents know that, if an ICO is made, the child is likely to be removed and may remain away for the rest of the proceedings. Usually these hearings are very early on in the process, so the court does not yet have all the evidence. It cannot yet be sure that the grounds for a full care order are met; instead it must be satisfied that there are 'reasonable grounds for believing' that they are. Making an ICO does not necessarily mean that a full care order will be made at the final hearing.

Often in practice the second and subsequent ICOs are made in a largely administrative hearing without anyone having to go to court.

Expert assessments

Sometimes the court needs an independent expert to carry out an assessment. This might be a psychiatric assessment of a parent's mental health, a second medical opinion (which may involve a further medical examination), or a psychological assessment of the functioning of one person or the family as a whole. Sometimes these assessments also involve the child. As foster carer, you may need to help in practical arrangements such as transporting the child to an assessment and of course supporting the child through the process.

Final hearing

Not all care proceedings end in a contested final hearing; many, even most, cases are settled and agreement reached between the parties at an earlier stage. The court must approve any such agreement and this is not simply a rubber stamp; the court must be satisfied that the agreement is in the child's best interests.

If the case is contested right up to the end, the final hearing may take several days. The written evidence presented by each party is considered, witnesses are called and cross-examined and the lawyers put their arguments about the facts and the law. Finally, the court delivers its judgment, detailing which facts it finds have been proven and reaching its conclusion.

Orders

It is up to the local authority to prove its case 'on the balance of probabilities' – that is to say that it is more likely than not that its version of events is the true one. Before a care order can be made, the court must:

- be satisfied that the 'threshold criteria' are met (that is, that there is actual or likely significant harm due to inadequate care or the child being out of control)

- remember that the child's welfare is paramount

- go through the list of factors in the 'welfare checklist'[2]

- decide that a care order is the most appropriate option from all the possible orders available

- consider the proposed care plan

- consider contact and whether an order is needed to regulate contact or to permit the local authority to refuse contact to a named person.

---

2   For more details, see pp.81–82.

Supervision orders

If the threshold criteria are met, the court could make a supervision order instead of a care order. The two orders are very different. A supervision order does not give the local authority PR, so it has no power to remove the child and no duty to accommodate and maintain him. Instead, the local authority's job is to 'advise, assist and befriend the child' for one year (which can later be extended to a maximum of three years in total).

The court also has the option of making other orders instead of a care order, such as a residence order, or it can decide not to make any order at all.

Placement orders

A local authority needs a placement order before it can place a child for adoption (except where a child is relinquished for adoption, when placement can go ahead with parental consent). Where the authority's care plan in care proceedings is for adoption, it should apply for the placement order at the same time as the care order.

> Jamie is two years old and subject to care proceedings. Borsetshire has thoroughly assessed his parents and ruled out rehabilitation. There are no family members or friends suitable and willing to care for him. Given Jamie's age, Borsetshire wants him to have the most secure, permanent future possible by finding him an adoptive family. All the complex administrative procedures are completed and Borsetshire applies for a placement order. This application is heard by the court at the same time as the application for a care order.
>
> The judge considers all the evidence and decides that Jamie suffered significant harm at the hands of his parents. He looks at all elements of Jamie's welfare and the options available to the court. He decides that adoption is the right care plan so makes a care order and a placement order. Jamie's social worker can start work immediately to find him an adoptive family.

After the hearing

After months of preparation and slow-moving proceedings, the final hearing arrives in a flurry of activity and before you know it the final order is made. In all the last-minute preparations it is important not to overlook planning for what happens when that decision is made, especially who is going to tell the child, how and where. If you are fostering a child going through care proceedings, you need to know this in advance and make sure you are told the outcome of the case and its implications as soon as possible. The last thing anyone wants is for a distraught mother to be the first person to tell the child that she is now in care forever, or for a triumphant father to tell the child that the court threw out the evidence and it was proved that he never touched her.

Depending on the circumstances and relationships, the right person to tell the child might be the social worker, Guardian, child's solicitor or a combination of the three. It is not a job for you as a foster carer, although it may well be appropriate for you to be present when the child is told. You also need to be prepared for any fall-out, from the child or the family, and to know what to do if there are problems. The first contact between child and family after the court case must also be carefully planned.

At the end of proceedings, there can sometimes be a feeling of anti-climax after months of focus on the case. The Guardian and the child's solicitor have no continuing role after the proceedings end, so they say goodbye to the child. Depending on how closely they have worked together and what sort of relationship has been established, this can sometimes be a loss for the child. The child, parents, social worker and foster carer have to get on with adjusting to the new legal situation and putting the plan into effect.

The foster carer's role in proceedings

During Georgia's care proceedings, her foster mum:
- carries on looking after Georgia day to day
- helps Georgia understand the proceedings and cope with the feelings they provoke
- welcomes Georgia's solicitor and Guardian whenever they want to see her in the foster home (never letting on how inconvenient the appointment is)

- encourages Georgia to talk openly to her solicitor and Guardian and helps her to contact them if she wants to talk

- makes sure the Guardian and solicitor spend enough time with Georgia and complains if they do not

- rearranges her schedule so she can transport Georgia to an expert assessment by a child psychologist, and copes with Georgia's feelings afterwards

- keeps in constant contact with Georgia's social worker and her own fostering support officer

- continues to keep a diary (the local authority's solicitor decides that this contains important evidence and asks her to make a statement and to come to court to give evidence[3]

- transports Georgia to and from court when she goes to see the judge and supports her through the process

- goes to court herself to give evidence

- plans with the social worker, solicitor and Guardian who is to tell Georgia the outcome and, with Georgia's agreement, sits in with the solicitor while he explains to her that the judge made a full care order so, against her wishes, Georgia must remain in foster care

- cares for and supports Georgia as she comes to terms with the decision

- fends off telephone calls from Georgia's distraught parents

- supports Georgia through the next very emotional contact with her parents

- works with Georgia and her social worker to plan for her future.

---

3   For more details on giving evidence, see Chapter 8.

Points for practice

- Make sure you understand enough about how care proceedings work in order to support a fostered child through the process.

- Be clear about the roles of the child's solicitor and Children's Guardian and be prepared to insist that the child receives the service she should from each of them.

- Advocate if necessary to ensure the child's wishes and feelings are properly represented.

- Make sure that proper plans are made to tell the child the outcome of proceedings.

- Make sure you are clear where you fit into the process. Get support of your own.

Chapter 8

The Foster Carer as Witness

To make the right decision for a child, the court needs all relevant information. Evidence in care proceedings is like a jigsaw puzzle – each piece on its own means nothing, but when all the pieces are put together, the picture emerges. If a child is or has been in foster care, information from the carers is part of that jigsaw.

Foster carers have important information about children – their physical condition, emotional state, behaviour, abilities and difficulties, relationships and reactions to contact. Often a carer's evidence shows change over time – perhaps a catch-up in growth or development, or patterns of behaviour – for example, the child has a bad day at school after every contact visit. Carers know the child better than any of the other professionals involved, so family courts often want to hear from them.

Keeping records

Memory is notoriously unreliable. Keeping records is a vital part of the discipline of the professional foster carer's role. All competent fostering agencies require carers to keep a daily diary or log book as part of the foster care agreement and many agencies provide a standard format for carers to use. Fostering officers should see diaries regularly and ensure that they are being kept properly.

Separate records should be kept for each fostered child, even siblings, because they may not always stay together. Remember confidentiality and ensure that personal information about one child does not go onto another child's records where it could be seen by people who have no right to see it.

The diary should record daily events including:

- health (any changes, illnesses, medication, medical examinations or treatment)

- behaviour (good or bad)

- education (attendance, progress, reports, school activities)

- significant or unusual events (good or bad)

- contact and reactions to it before, during or after contact

- any dealings with the child's parents

- significant comments made by the child

- activities and achievements

- emotional state.

Recording facts

Stick to facts – who, what, when, where – and avoid opinion or speculation. Leave it to others – social workers, psychologists or the court – to draw conclusions about what the facts mean.

> Kate fosters Leanne, who is seven years old and normally a lively child. Leanne sees her parents every Tuesday afternoon. After contact, she is unusually quiet and subdued and every Tuesday night she wets the bed although she is dry the rest of the time.
> Kate writes in her diary one Wednesday:
>
>> Leanne wet the bed again last night. She always does this after contact. I think seeing her mum and dad reminds her of all the terrible things that happened at home and she worries that she'll have to go back to them.
>
> Kate is called to give evidence in Leanne's care proceedings. Her diary is copied to all the parties. When she is in the witness box, the parents' barrister cross-examines Kate. He asks her what psychological qualifications she has. When Kate says she has none, he asks her what gives her the right to analyse why Leanne wets the bed. Then he suggests that perhaps Leanne wets the bed because she is upset at having to leave her parents and wishes she could go home. Kate has to accept that this is possible. Then the barrister

accuses Kate of being biased and argues that all her evidence should be treated with caution because she is judgmental. He even suggests that Kate might be trying to turn Leanne against her parents.

He could not have scored any of these points if Kate had just stuck to the facts and let the court decide on all the evidence why Leanne wets the bed.

Facts are often more powerful evidence than opinions, especially in subjective matters like hygiene, cleanliness and behaviour – what one person thinks is appalling might seem fine to someone else. Birth families often think that foster families impose their own excessively high standards and often protest that they too could provide more if they only had a fostering allowance.

Mikey has been physically neglected. On the day he arrives in foster care, his carer Nicky could write in her diary:

Mikey was filthy, his clothes were inappropriate and he was in a disgusting state.

Or she could write:

Mikey arrived wearing a short-sleeved T-shirt and shorts although it was a cold day. His T-shirt was marked aged 2–4 but Mikey is six years old. It was so tight that it left a red mark around his neck when I took it off him. His whole body was dirty, not just his arms, legs and face and he needed a thorough bath. His hair was long and so knotted and matted that I could not comb it so I had to cut the knots out.

Which gives a clearer picture? Which would you find more helpful if you were the judge?

Sometimes it is difficult to distinguish between fact and opinion: opinions do not have to start with phrases like 'in my opinion' or 'I think'. If, for example, a carer says a child is 'disturbed' or a parent was 'drunk', these may look like facts but actually they are opinions, conclusions drawn from the facts (the father was unsteady on his feet, his speech was slurred and so on). Be aware of whether you are offering facts or interpretation, and try to stick to facts.

The court only accepts opinion evidence from experts because these are the only opinions that actually help the court. Expertise can be established by qualifications or experience.

Nina has been fostering for 40 years, caring for babies who are relinquished for adoption. She has cared for 30 babies from newborn to six months old. Although Nina has no academic qualifications, she has enormous experience of young babies so when she describes Olivia as 'exceptionally difficult to feed' and as having 'an unusually piercing cry' the court listens carefully to these views. Nina is not a doctor: she cannot diagnose the cause of the problem. However, she can tell the court that she has cared for ten babies diagnosed as addicted to heroin at birth and Olivia had similar difficulties. She can offer the court her experience, but she must not cross the line and claim medical expertise. Knowing your boundaries is an important part of professionalism in foster care.

Balance

We know that children are usually in foster care because of difficulties in the family so we can tend to focus on problems because these seem to be what is relevant to the court case. In fact this is not so: positives are just as important as negatives to give the court the full picture.

Do not worry that too many positives might seem to undermine the social worker's case: it is not your job to put any sort of gloss on the information – just say it like it is.

The social worker's evidence is that Olly's father, Pete, is abusive and unco-operative. But Olly's foster carer, Quinlan, has no problem with Pete – in fact, they get on well. Pete co-operates over contact and regularly telephones to see how Olly is.

This goes into Quinlan's records and eventually into a court statement. It might seem to contradict the social worker's case, but the court needs the whole picture and it is certainly not Quinlan's job to edit the information to make it fit. The court understands that it is perfectly possible for Pete to behave differently towards different professionals in the case.

Try to give the court as much relevant information about positives as about negatives.

Ravi fosters Sanjay, whose behaviour can be very challenging. On difficult days, Ravi's diary entries are long detailed accounts of everything that has happened. This is very useful to the court. However, on other days, Ravi's diary entry often simply reads 'Sanjay had a good day today' and the rest of the page is blank. We might understand why Ravi breathes a sigh of relief on a good day, but the court would like to know what was good about it in order to get the balanced picture. And if one day Sanjay reads the diary he will find reams about how terrible he was but almost nothing about how good and loveable he could be.

Mind your language!

Always keep your language detached, neutral and professional. This is not your personal diary, it is a record for the child. It is not the place to let off steam or express your personal views about the child, his parents or his social worker – do that elsewhere.

Remember who might read your diary, including the child (possibly years from now), the parents, legal representatives and a judge. Re-read what you write to make sure nothing is going to embarrass you or seem unfair, judgmental, offensive or insensitive.

Recording what the child says

Children often talk to their foster carers, revealing significant details about life at home or expressing their wishes and feelings. Try to write down the child's own words wherever possible, not your interpretation of them. Details about the context, the child's behaviour and demeanour at the time can help.

Sometimes the first time a child feels safe enough to disclose abuse is when settled in a foster home and confiding in a trusted carer. For more about recording and managing disclosures, see Chapter 16.

Writing a court statement

In care proceedings, all evidence is recorded in statements and reports that are copied to everyone involved in the case and read by the court before the hearing takes place. These proceedings centre on a child's welfare, so there is no room for surprise revelations from the witness box.

The local authority's lawyer may ask you for a copy of your diary and a statement of evidence. Practice varies: lawyers may ask you to write the statement yourself, or they may interview you and prepare a draft statement for you. Statements for court must be in a set form: the local authority lawyer will make sure your statement includes all the correct formalities.

Never put your name to a statement unless you are completely happy with it – remember it will be you, not the local authority's lawyer, standing in the witness box answering questions about it.

Make sure your statement is:

- accurate – check every single fact

- balanced and fair, including positives as well as negatives

- written in jargon-free plain English in a professional tone, neither pompous nor casual, avoiding emotion and judgment

- factual, avoiding opinion and speculation

- complete, giving the court all the relevant information you have to help it make the right decision for the child

- easy to read, well laid-out and divided into manageable sections

- free from grammatical errors and spelling mistakes

- a professional document that says exactly what you want it to say.

If a lawyer drafts the statement for you, do not sign it until you are completely happy with every word, not just what it says but how it says it.

If you are preparing your own statement, make sure your fostering officer works on it with you before sending it on.

Preparing for court

Not everyone who submits a statement in care proceedings has to go to court. If agreement is reached, no-one has to give evidence in court. Even when a case remains contested, often the evidence of some witnesses is accepted. If no-one challenges your statement, you do not have to go to court – judges do not waste time listening to information they have already read in a statement and which is not disputed.

However, if you have written a statement, always work on the assumption that you will have to go to court.

Practical preparations

Where? Know where you are going (there is often more than one court in the same town), how to get there, how long it takes and where to park (few courts have car parks). Once you get to the court building, know where you will meet your legal team.

When? Know the date and time of the hearing. Be prepared for a long wait while other cases are heard, negotiations are going on or other witnesses are giving evidence – take something with you to keep yourself occupied. Court hearings usually finish at 4pm but this is never guaranteed – have contingency plans in place for who will pick the children up from school and prepare dinner if you are late home.

Who? Know who will meet you at court, remembering it may be someone you have never met before.

Why? Be clear exactly why you are going to court, what your role is and what to expect. Lawyers who ask you to come to court cannot rehearse your evidence, but they can give you an idea of the sorts of questions you might be asked. Re-read your statement before attending court. Look the part – professional and respectable.

As well as practical preparations, seek professional support from your fostering officer and emotional support from those around you. You are bound to be nervous (it would be worrying if you were not – over-confident witnesses are dangerous), so have support in place to help you through this professional challenge.

Giving oral evidence

Witnesses are not allowed to hear other evidence before their own turn in the witness box, so you have to wait outside the courtroom until you are called. The usher calls your name, shows you into the courtroom and your evidence starts straight away. The judge or magistrates, advocates and parties (including the child's parents) are already in their places. Since April 2009 members of the press may also be present, although there are strict limitations on what they can report.

> **Tip**
> Get to court early and ask the usher (who wears a black gown) to show you inside the courtroom, show you where the witness box is and explain who sits where. This will give you more confidence when you walk in to give your evidence.

When you take your place in the witness box, you are asked to remain standing and take the oath or the affirmation. Both are solemn promises to tell the truth, the whole truth and nothing but the truth. The oath is sworn on the Bible or other holy book, while the affirmation is non-religious. Both are of equal value. The usher will either show you a card printed with the words of the oath or affirmation and ask you to read them aloud, or she will say the correct words and ask you to repeat them after her. Once you are on oath, you cannot discuss the case with anyone until your evidence is finished and if you lie you can be prosecuted for perjury.

> **Tip**
> Know in advance whether you want to swear or affirm. If you want to swear on any holy book other than the New Testament, let the usher know in advance so that she can find the right book and the right form of words.

In the FPC, everyone remains seated during proceedings so, once you are sworn in, you will be asked to sit. In the County Court and High Court, witnesses usually remain standing. Then the local authority's lawyer will ask you some questions. This stage is called 'examination in chief' and is very brief. You will be asked to confirm your name and address – do not give your home address if the placement is a confidential one.

Tips

The early stages of giving evidence are relatively straightforward – the words of the oath are there for you and, however nervous you feel, you will remember your own name and address. Use these early stages to calm your nerves and get used to addressing the court.

- Speak up – make sure everyone can hear you.

- Don't speak too quickly – people need to take notes of your evidence.

- Face the judge or magistrates and look at them when you are giving your answers. Do this right from the start when you take the oath. Point your feet and body towards them, so that you naturally face them to give your answers even if the questions come from someone else. This is the single most powerful technique of an effective witness because:

  ○ the judge or magistrates are the people who really need to know what you are saying – they are making the decision – so talk to them

  ○ looking at them means you are not looking at the advocate asking you questions – a definite advantage if you feel pressured under cross-examination

  ○ you might get some feedback through their expression or body language (but don't worry if they give nothing away).

Next you will probably be asked to look in the 'bundle', a complete paginated set of all the papers in the case – applications, orders, statements and reports – in a lever-arch file. You will be asked to turn to your own statement, to confirm that it is your statement and your signature, and that the contents are true to the best of your knowledge and belief. Once you have done that, it is as if you had given all that evidence on oath in the witness box – you do not have to say it all again.

> **Tip**
> If when you re-read your statement before court you find an error, this is the moment to draw it to the court's attention and correct it.

That is probably the end of examination in chief, except perhaps to bring things up to date since you wrote your statement (although anything significant should have gone into an updating statement). Next it is time for cross-examination.

Cross-examination

This is the opportunity for the respondents' lawyers (parents, child and Children's Guardian) each to ask questions from their own clients' perspective. They probe the evidence with two objectives in mind:

1. undermining the local authority's case, and

2. establishing their own client's case.

In cross-examination, lawyers might aim to show that you are:

- lying or 'mistaken'

- incompetent

- selective, giving the court only the bits of information that suit

- biased, judgmental, hostile to the parents or motivated to keep the child for yourself

- straying beyond your role, giving opinions you are not qualified to give.

Witnesses often assume that cross-examination will be hostile and unpleasant. This is often not so, especially in family courts where there is no jury to impress and where the court focuses on the child's welfare. Often, questions are asked in an apparently mild, even sympathetic way. Don't be lulled into a false sense of security – the 'friendly' opponent can be just as dangerous as the hostile one.

Tips

- Remember that this is not personal and you are not on trial. Put yourself in the parents' shoes – if you were in danger of losing your child wouldn't you use every argument and tactic you possibly could? Don't be surprised if the parents do exactly that.

- Don't rush into answers. Take your time, take a deep breath, consider the question and think about your answer.

- If you don't hear the question, don't understand it or don't know the answer, say so.

- Stick to your role and boundaries – don't be tempted to 'help out' by straying beyond your limits.

- Stay cool, calm and collected – never lose your temper.

- Don't get too relaxed – never forget you are giving evidence on oath in a case about a child's future.

- Always remember that you are there for the child.

The final stage of your evidence is re-examination, when the local authority's lawyer can ask questions following up on anything raised in cross-examination. Usually there are very few questions, if any.

The judge or magistrates can ask questions at any time. Judges are more likely to ask questions whenever they arise while magistrates often wait until the end of the witness's evidence. If it is a Bench of lay magistrates, questions are asked by the Chair, who sits in the middle.

When your evidence is complete, provided you are told you are free to leave, your role is over and the rest of the case continues with other witnesses being called, the lawyers making their closing submissions and eventually the court announcing its decision and reasons.

After court

As well as ensuring you and the child are told quickly and appropriately about the outcome and its implications, make sure that you get feedback on your evidence. Ask for an objective view of how things went, to build on positives and improve on weaknesses for next time.

Points for practice

- Always keep a separate diary for each fostered child.

- Make sure you know how to keep records and what should and should not go in the diary – if you are unclear, seek training.

- Critically review your diary now and then – are your records appropriate?

- Make sure you understand the key elements of writing a statement for court. Take advice and seek support if you are asked to write a statement. Never sign a statement unless you are happy with every single word.

- Make sure you are properly prepared if you are asked to give evidence in court. Insist on advice, support and feedback.

Chapter 9

Duties towards Looked After Children

According to government statistics, there are some 61,000 looked after children in England and nearly 5000 in Wales at any one time.[1] Around 59 per cent of them are subject to care orders. As High Court judge Munby LJ said in the High Court:

> The State assumes a heavy burden when it takes a child into care… If the State is to justify removing children from their parents, it can only be on the basis that the State is going to provide a better quality of care than that from which the child has been rescued.[2]

Unfortunately we know that looked after children often do less well than their counterparts, achieving less educationally and more likely to be excluded from school or in trouble with the law. The objective of improving outcomes for looked after children has led to a plethora of initiatives.

Foster carers play a crucial role: as well as caring day to day for most looked after children, they are there to ensure that services are provided and plans made appropriately, and to advocate for their young charges.

---

1   Figures as at 31 March 2009. Available for England at www.dcsf.gov.uk/rsgateway/DB/SFR/s000878/index.shtml, accessed on 6 July 2010.
    Available for Wales at www.wales.gov.uk/docs/statistics/2009/090826sdr127200 9en.pdf?lang=eng, accessed on 6 July 2010.
2   *Re F; F v Lambeth LBC* [2002] 1FLR 217, High Court, paragraph 43. Munby LJ is now a Court of Appeal judge.

Local authority's duties to looked after children

A local authority must:

- 'safeguard and promote' the welfare of looked after children

- provide them with accommodation

- otherwise maintain them.

The local authority must consider the various placement options available and choose the most appropriate one for the child in all the circumstances. Rehabilitation to parents is the first choice, or, if that is not possible, placement with family or friends. An alternative placement could be in a children's home or supported lodgings, but most looked after children are in foster care.

Placement considerations
LOCATION
Under CA89, the placement should be near the child's home provided that is reasonably practicable and consistent with the child's welfare. The Children and Young Persons Act 2008 strengthens the CA89 by including a presumption that the accommodation should be within the local authority's own area, near the child's home and not disrupting the child's education (especially if GCSEs are approaching). Under the Care Planning, Placement and Case Review Regulations (England) 2010 ('the Care Planning Regulations'),[3] decisions to place a child out of area will have to be made by the Director of Children's Services or his nominee. This is backed up by a duty on local authorities to ensure that they have a sufficient supply of accommodation to meet looked after children's needs, in terms of diversity as well as numbers.

> Eleven-year-old Alfie is in the care of Norminster because he was putting himself at extreme risk from his behaviour, mixing with adults who involved him in crime, drug taking and prostitution. Alfie's social workers believe that, if they place him locally, he will still be at risk from these people. They make a deliberate choice to place him in foster care in rural Borsetshire, 80 miles from home, for his own welfare. This is a genuine exception to the normal policy.

---

3   Expected to be brought into force on 1 April 2011.

Ben is in the care of Newtonshire where there has been a mass exodus of disaffected foster carers from the local authority to Supercarers. The Area Director refuses to contract with Supercarers because the agency has poached his carers. This means there are no carers locally for Ben, so he is placed with carers from Valuecare 120 miles from home. Ben is effectively cut off from his family, friends and school for no valid reason. This is not consistent with his welfare and is not justified under CA89.

SIBLINGS

There is a strong statutory presumption that siblings should stay together whenever reasonably practicable and consistent with their welfare. We must not underestimate the importance of sibling relationships: siblings have often been through difficult experiences together, understand each other like no-one else and it will probably be the longest relationship of a lifetime. However, each child's needs must be considered overall and this can cause complications.

Connor and Delia are taken into care because of sexual abuse. They are very close and at first they are placed together, but the carer observes that their play together is very sexualised. After careful consideration, it is decided that they would be better placed separately.

Elvis (2), Eric (4), Ernie (6), Edwina (8), Eliza (10) and Erica (12) are all removed from home in an emergency. A placement for them all together cannot be found immediately. The three girls are placed together in one foster home, Eric and Ernie in another and Elvis in a third. In the circumstances, this is all that is 'reasonably practicable', and it is acceptable in the short term. However, over time, the placements become fixed. Elvis, who is readily adoptable, ends up going for adoption on his own, separated permanently from his siblings. Eric and Ernie go to another adoptive placement, while the girls remain fostered long term. What was 'reasonably practicable' in an emergency became a long-term plan by default without proper analysis: the long-term pairings were effectively decided by the availability of foster homes on the first night. This is not proper care planning for any of the children.

Frankie and Freddy are half-brothers, removed from their mother. Rehabilitation to her is impossible. Frankie's father is assessed as suitable for him but he is not interested in Freddy, whose father is unknown. Unfortunately the boys' interests conflict: it is in Frankie's best interests to live with his dad, even if this means separation from

Freddy. There is always a strong presumption that a child should live with an available parent. However, for Freddy, it would be best to stay with Frankie. It is not possible to meet both boys' needs. Frankie goes to live with his dad while Freddy remains in foster care. The best that can be done for Freddy is to ensure regular contact with his brother.

CHILDREN WITH DISABILITIES

When a child with a disability is looked after, the local authority's duty is 'so far as is reasonably practicable' to place him in accommodation which is 'not unsuitable' for his particular needs. This duty will be strengthened to providing accommodation that is positively suitable when the Children and Young Persons Act 2008 is fully in force.

RACE, CULTURE, RELIGION AND LANGUAGE

The local authority must give 'due consideration' to a child's racial origin, cultural and linguistic background and religious persuasion whenever it makes a decision for a looked after child. Linguistic background includes languages that are signed rather than spoken.

Local authorities must by law consider the cultural diversity of their area when recruiting foster carers, in order to provide suitable carers for children who become looked after. That does not mean that children cannot or should never be placed with foster carers from a different background – sometimes other needs outweigh those arising from a child's heritage – but these factors must always be considered when trying to find the best available 'match'. If some of a child's needs are not met by the placement, thought must be given to how to fill the gap through services, support or training.

All foster carers should receive training to raise their general awareness and understanding of cultural and diversity issues and equal opportunities. You should always feel empowered to ask for the training you need on issues raised by a particular child's placement: agencies must by law provide the training carers need in the interests of the children they are looking after. Training is not limited to a fixed curriculum – it might include learning a language or signing system, or learning about hair care or make-up for a teenage girl from a different ethnic background.

Cultural factors are not just important in finding a suitable placement: they must be considered throughout the child's time as a looked after child and beyond. Make sure these elements of the child's identity are properly considered.

CONFIDENTIALITY

By law parents (including a father without PR) and anyone else with PR should normally be informed of the child's placement address. However, this can be kept confidential if the child is in care (not voluntarily accommodated) and the local authority has reasonable cause to believe that informing the person concerned would prejudice the child's welfare – for example, cases where there is a risk of violence or attempted abduction. 'Welfare' also includes the child's emotional and psychological well-being – for example, a sexually abused teenager may feel safer if her abusive father does not know where she is.

The child's role

Before making any decision for a child who is (or is about to be) looked after, the local authority must by law ascertain the child's wishes and feelings, as far as reasonably practicable. This should be done in an appropriate way considering the child's age and development: some children may express themselves non-verbally and need an advocate's help to put their views across.

These wishes and feelings must be considered in any decisions, having regard to the child's age and understanding. This, of course, is not the same as saying that the authority must follow the child's wishes – sometimes what children want is not what, objectively, is good for them – for example, in one case the High Court found that a local authority had given too much weight to the wishes of a teenager who was out of control and set on self-destruction. If a decision goes against the child's wishes, this needs to be explained, along with information about how to complain or take the matter further.[4]

Lack of co-operation

Lack of co-operation (from anyone – parents, other agencies or children themselves) never absolves local authorities from their legal duties. Finding

---

4   For more details on possible legal action, see p. 126–7.

creative ways to engage young people is part of the challenge of social work and, as the child's carer, you may be able to aid communication or suggest approaches as well as pressing for social workers to take the time to work with a child. The High Court judge Munby LJ said in a case about a young man who refused to co-operate in devising his pathway plan:

> The fact that a child is unco-operative and unwilling to engage, or even refuses to engage, is no reason for the local authority not to carry out its obligations under the Act and the Regulations. After all, a disturbed child's unwillingness to engage with those who are trying to help is often merely a part of the overall problem which justified the local authority's statutory intervention in the first place. The local authority must do its best.[5]

Even quite extreme behaviour does not justify excluding young people from their legal right (guaranteed under the Human Rights Act 1998) to be properly informed and consulted about fundamentally important decisions. The Court of Appeal found that one 14-year-old mother, who was in care herself, should have been consulted before the plan for her baby was changed from keeping them together to a plan of adoption – even though she had made serious threats of violence to her foster mother and, when she was told of the plan to remove her baby, assaulted the social worker and police officer.[6]

The parents' role

The local authority also has to consult parents before making any decisions for looked after children to ascertain their wishes and feelings, so far as practicable, and to take these into account. This duty is not limited to parents with PR – fathers without PR are also included, as are people who have PR but who are not parents.

---

5   *R(J) v Caerphilly CBC* [2005] EWHC 586 Admin at para 56, High Court. Munby LJ is now a Court of Appeal judge.

6   *Re C (Breach of Human Rights: Damages)* [2007] EWCA Civ 2, Court of Appeal.

Other relevant people

Before taking decisions for a looked after child, the local authority must also find out the views of 'any other person whose wishes and feelings the authority consider to be relevant'. This includes foster carers – indeed, it is hard to think of anyone more relevant than the person actually looking after the child. As a foster carer, you should have an important role in the planning for the child, whom you probably know better than any of the other professionals involved. You also have a realistic view of the likely practical impact of any decision on the child's day-to-day life.

> Jordan is eight and in foster care, and his brother is placed separately. His parents' relationship was violent and they cannot have contact together. The social worker proposes contact with his brother twice a week, each parent twice a week and grandparents once a week. It is left to his foster carer to point out that this makes seven contact visits a week. Jordan also goes to therapy once a week and to Cubs, which he adores. He is in danger of being passed around like a parcel from one contact to the next, with no time to relax or play with friends or simply enjoy the normal family life that is an important part of foster care. The social worker accepts that Jordan's needs overall have to be considered.

Care orders and care plans

Before a court makes a final care order, it must consider the local authority's care plan explaining how it proposes to look after the child. This includes:

- the overall aim and timescale
- the child's needs
- how these are to be met
- proposed placement
- health and education plans
- contact
- parents' and child's views
- contingency plan
- details of who within the authority is responsible for putting the plan into effect.

The court cannot dictate the care plan, but if it is unhappy with the proposed plan it could refuse to make a care order or make other orders instead.

Residence order

Gregory is subject to care proceedings. His grandmother Hannah wants to care for him, but the local authority rejected her application and proposes foster care for Gregory. The judge decides that Gregory should live with Hannah. He can achieve this by making a residence order to Hannah instead of a care order.

Contact order

The local authority seeks a care order for Ian and proposes to offer Ian's parents limited supervised contact. The judge decides that there should be more contact. He makes an order specifying contact alongside the care order.

Adjournment for reflection

Jack is placed with foster carers Mr and Mrs Kennedy under an ICO and is thriving. However, as they are approved as short-term carers, the care plan is to move Jack to another placement. The judge agrees that a full care order is the only option for Jack, but he would like him to stay with the Kennedys. They are happy to keep Jack as a foster child, but they do not want a residence order. There is no other order within the court's armoury to dictate the care plan so that Jack can stay put. The judge adjourns the final decision for a week asking the local authority to re-think the care plan and, if it is not changed so that Jack can remain where he is long term, the Director of Children's Services must come to court to explain why. If the local authority sticks to its guns and refuses to change the plan, the judge has no alternative but to express his annoyance and make the care order. But it is to be hoped that both local authority and court with Jack's best interests at heart will find a way forward.

Accommodated children and care plans

What about children who are accommodated voluntarily? There is no court to demand and scrutinise a care plan for them. The local authority must by law ascertain children's wishes and feelings, and take these into account before accommodating them. Their foster placement agreement or placement plan sets out detailed arrangements and many accommodated children already have a core assessment to inform plans for them. From 1 April 2011 when the Care Planning Regulations come into force, children in England who are voluntarily accommodated will have to have a detailed care plan, just like their counterparts who are in care.

Planning for permanence

Care planning must consider the longer term as well as the child's immediate needs. Drift has been the curse of looked after children for too long. Every plan should have an objective for permanence – rehabilitation to the child's birth family or, if that is not possible, adoption or long-term foster care to adulthood. Plans should also include a contingency – a plan B in case plan A does not work out.

Health care

All looked after children must have a medical assessment before or as soon as practicable after becoming looked after. Thereafter, they should have regular medicals (every six months for younger children and annually for older children), although competent children can refuse to be examined.

Local authorities must arrange medical and dental care for looked after children. The child's Personal Health Plan includes mental and physical health, and preventive care such as immunisations. In general, the local authority should act as a responsible parent would. In practice, of course, much of the responsibility for ensuring that appointments are kept and health needs are met falls to foster carers.

Education

To date, being looked after has sadly been associated with educational underachievement. The significance of education for children's life chances cannot be overstated, so for looked after children proper educational provision is vital. All looked after children should have a

Personal Education Plan (PEP) specifying what needs to be done and by whom to help them meet their potential. The PEP reflects any existing education plan such as a Statement of Special Educational Needs. The child's education history, attendance and discipline record, academic progress and achievement, and any special needs, support or provision all form part of the PEP.

It is essential to plan in partnership with education professionals – the child's school, including the designated teacher responsible for looked after children, or education officers for those not in school. Proper provision for excluded children is crucial. As ever, foster carers have vital input into devising the PEP and a key role in putting it into practice. Support or practical assistance for carers should also form part of the plan.

Pathway plans

For teenagers, advance planning for moving towards independence is vitally important. This is considered further in Chapter 18.

Social work visits

The child's social worker should visit within one week of the placement, then at least every six weeks for the first year and every three months thereafter. The social worker should see the child alone, unless the child refuses, and prepare a report on each visit recording the child's views and assessing how the placement is meeting the child's needs. These are of course minimum requirements and social workers should visit as often as needed and whenever reasonably requested by the child or the carer. Foster carers may need to be assertive to ensure that social workers visit fostered children as they should. Visits should not be neglected just because the placement seems to be going well.

Reviews

Things change, life moves on. For looked after children just as for the rest of us, what looked like a good plan at the time may not work in practice. Everything has to be kept under review. For looked after children, this is a formal process. Every looked after child's case must be reviewed within four weeks of the child becoming looked after, the second review within three months after that and thereafter at least every six months. These are minimum periods, and reviews should be held whenever necessary and brought forward if there are unexpected developments.

Purpose of reviews

Reviews are to look at what has happened since the last meeting to see where things now stand – how is the child doing, is the placement meeting the child's needs, are necessary services in place and are they working – and to decide where to go from here. Sometimes this means a major reassessment: for example, if a planned rehabilitation has failed, the whole objective of the plan may need to change. In other cases, the overall objective remains sound but the means of achieving it need to change. Sometimes the child is reaching a new developmental stage and plans have to be made for a looked after child as for any other child – for example, which secondary school to go to. Sometimes all is going well and everything can carry on unchanged until the next review.

It is important that reviews are taken very seriously – it is not just a question of holding a meeting on time and ticking boxes.

Who takes part in a review?

The review needs input from everyone with relevant information – professionals and family members – but not everyone needs to attend the meeting, which could otherwise become unwieldy and intimidating especially for the child. Some people can contribute in writing or in a meeting before the review.

The most important input of all should come from the children themselves, whether or not they wish to attend the meeting. Time and effort needs to be put in to help them contribute.

Parents and other relevant family members should participate in the review and the decision-making process as appropriate – sometimes it is not appropriate for parents to attend, but their views should be sought and presented to the meeting.

Foster carers have vital information and views to contribute to reviews, and should be fully involved.

The review considers:

- whether decisions at the last review have been implemented and, if they have, their outcome and if they haven't, why not

- changes in circumstances since the last review

- whether the placement remains appropriate

- educational progress and how the PEP is meeting the child's needs

- leisure activities and interests, and whether current arrangements are appropriate

- health (physical and emotional), the outcome of the most recent health assessment and whether the health plan is meeting the child's needs

- identity needs – religion, race, culture, etc. – and how these are being met

- planning for permanence

- whether the child's legal status remains appropriate or should be changed (e.g. should a care order be discharged, or should an accommodated child become subject to care proceedings?)

- contact

- planning towards when the child ceases to be looked after (whether moving towards independence or being discharged from accommodation or care).

There is no point making decisions unless they will be implemented, so allocating responsibility for action together with a timescale is crucial. There should be a written record of all reviews.

The Independent Reviewing Officer (IRO)

IROs were created because of judicial frustration and anger that care plans were not being implemented. In one case, two boys drifted in care for eight years with no care plan. The High Court described this as 'scandalous' and the local authority's 'dereliction of duty' as 'shaming'. In another case a local authority presented the court with an apparently beautifully constructed care plan putting in various services and therapy to lead to rehabilitation within six to nine months. In fact none of those services were provided and rehabilitation did not happen. The case went all the way to the House of Lords (the highest court in the land)[7] where the judges expressed their frustration that courts had no power to ensure that care plans were actually implemented. They urged Parliament to change the system: IROs were the result.

THE IRO'S ROLE

An IRO must be a qualified and experienced social worker, independent of line management or budgetary responsibility. Currently, IROs remain within the local authority but the government has a power (in reserve until 2015) to transfer them to an independent body, presumably if the current structure proves ineffective.

Each child should have a named IRO allocated to the case. Make sure you have your child's IRO's contact details. The IRO's job is to:

- ensure that reviews happen when they should and are brought forward if necessary

- see the child and make sure his views are heard, however they are expressed and whatever his age or ability, providing whatever assistance the child needs to express himself

- ensure the review has the information it needs and the right people attend

- chair the review meeting

- keep the review child and family centred

- make sure the care plan names those responsible for implementing decisions

- ensure the plan is carried out

- complete the review record, evaluating the plan

- notify senior managers if a child's case is not reviewed on time or if decisions are not carried through

- identify and report on good and bad practice

- address any problems with the plan.

---

7   At that time – since replaced by the Supreme Court.

The IRO should be notified of any significant changes in circumstances between reviews or if agreed action is not implemented – the IRO may then bring the next review forward or take other action.

Make sure that the IRO is kept informed and that the role is being performed properly.

TACKLING PROBLEMS

IROs have an important role. They may be the first port of call if a child is unhappy or if you as a carer feel that the plan is not the right one or promised services are not being delivered. The IRO should take matters up the line, right to Chief Executive level if necessary, to try to resolve problems.

IROs also have a duty to ensure that everyone is aware of the procedure for representations and complaints, which the local authority must have under CA89. This is open to children, their parents, others with PR, foster carers and anyone else with a sufficient connection to the child. Children are entitled to independent advocates to help them make complaints.[8]

If all else fails, legal action may be necessary, especially if a child's human rights may be being breached. IROs can help children obtain legal advice if they are competent and want to take legal action, or they can see if an adult (possibly a carer) is willing to act on a child's behalf, or, if there is no-one else to take action, they must refer the matter to CAFCASS who may take action on the child's behalf.

EXAMPLES OF LEGAL ACTION

S's case[9]

S was accommodated when she was 14. She had moderate learning difficulties and was extremely vulnerable – self-harming, abusing drugs and alcohol, and being sexually exploited. She gave birth to a baby and care proceedings followed in respect of the baby. The Official Solicitor represented S in those proceedings (because S was a parent in care proceedings and not competent to instruct a solicitor herself). He was so shocked at S's history that he took legal action on her behalf, claiming

---

8   Under s26A CA89.

9   *S (by the Official Solicitor) v Rochdale MBC and another (Independent Reviewing Officer)* [2008] EWHC 3283.

her rights to protection from harm and to have a fair trial had been breached. He complained that:

- there had been no assessment of S's psychological functioning

- there was no assessment of special educational needs and no PEP

- there was no pathway plan

- a referral to CAMHS had not been followed through

- records were inadequate

- reviews were·treated as a 'tick box' exercise instead of occasions for proper review and planning

- S's IRO had been 'largely impotent or supine'

- S did not have a qualified social worker.

S's legal status should have been reviewed: being accommodated had left her disadvantaged, partly due to the authority's policy of allocating unqualified workers to accommodated children. There were clear grounds for care proceedings; had these been started earlier, S and her mother would have been legally represented and proper assessments would have been carried out. If S had not given birth to a baby, none of the deficiencies in her own care would have come to light.

CD's case[10]

CD was a 15-year-old girl with quadriplegic cerebral palsy and registered blind. For ten years, her support package included regular respite care with the same foster carers, sometimes for five nights a week. However, the foster home was not and could not be made suitable for her changing needs. The carers wanted to move to a more suitable property and asked for the local authority's support. Instead, the local authority changed the plan – against the strong wishes of the child, her mother and the carers – to a placement for four nights a week at a boarding school and one weekend a month at a residential unit. The case went for judicial review to the High Court, which declared the plan to be unlawful. The local authority was told to re-consider, taking proper account of the child's clear and consistent wishes and her strong relationship with the carers (promoted by the local authority over the previous ten years).

---

10   *R(CD) v Isle of Anglesey County Council* [2005] 1FLR 59, High Court.

T's case[11]

T was a 14-year-old boy, a victim and perpetrator of sexual abuse, excluded from school and involved in violence, drug abuse, theft and arson. A thorough risk assessment recommended a specialist residential placement. Instead, a plan was made to place him in a children's home (previously judged unsuitable) and in mainstream schooling. The High Court ruled this to be irrational and unreasonable; it did not take account of the boy's wishes and feelings, inter-agency working had failed, the plan was based on inadequate information and was fundamentally flawed. There should have been sound reasons for not following the risk assessment.

LEGAL OPTIONS

Applications under CA89

Leila is in care. The plan is for her to be rehabilitated to the care of her mother Maggie but none of the promised work has been done. Leila (or someone on her behalf) or Maggie could apply to court for the care order to be discharged or, if it is too soon for that, for an order for increased contact including regular overnight stays.

Judicial review

Neil is accommodated. He has no care plan, reviews are not held on time and his case is drifting without direction. He complained to his IRO who achieved nothing, and he went through the local authority's complaints procedure without success. He can seek judicial review from the High Court because the local authority is breaching its statutory duty. The High Court could direct the authority to act.

Action for breach of human rights

Oscar has been with foster carers from Supercarers for four years. He is well settled and thriving. The local authority has a budget crisis and needs to cut costs. The Director of Children's Services instructs staff to move all looked after children from IFAs back

---

11   *Re T (Judicial Review: Local Authority Decisions Concerning Child in Need)* [2003] EWHC 2515 (Admin) [2004] 6011 FLR High Court.

into local authority placements. Oscar is distraught. He can seek judicial review to quash a decision made without following proper procedures and to take action for breach of his human rights – his right to a fair trial, because he has not been consulted, and his right to a family life because his carers, although not his birth family, are his psychological family.

GETTING LEGAL ADVICE

The child or someone on his behalf should consult a solicitor who is a member of the Law Society's Children Panel (showing accredited expertise in children's law), the Children's Legal Centre[12] or NYAS (the National Youth Advocacy Service).[13] Legal Aid may be available.

Points for practice

- Always know the name and contact details of every fostered child's IRO.

- Make sure you and your fostered children are properly consulted in planning.

- Are reviews a useful exercise for your fostered child? If not, discuss with the IRO what needs to change.

- Do your fostered children have proper care plans that meet their needs? If not, be prepared to take the matter further.

- Make sure you know what you and your fostered child can do to challenge or complain about a decision or service.

---

12   www.childrenslegalcentre.com.
13   www.nyas.net.

Chapter 10

Contact

Contact is one of the most important elements of a care plan.

What is contact for?

This is the key question, yet it often seems to be overlooked in the complicated process of balancing competing claims, making compromises and making practical arrangements. But unless we know what contact is for, how can we possibly decide the right type and level of contact? Failure to focus on this key issue sometimes results in contact being decided by the availability of a room or a supervisor. Some children miss out on contact with adults who work because resources are only available on weekdays. This happens because planning is done backwards, fitting needs to resources, when we should decide what is needed, then find the resources to make it possible.

In some cases, contact may be working towards rehabilitation to a parent, building up gradually towards ever longer staying contact. In the meantime, contact with other people in the child's life might have to take a back seat.

Where rehabilitation is not the plan, contact has the different purpose of maintaining links and preserving the child's sense of identity.

Sometimes the appropriate contact is no contact at all.

Who is contact for?

Primarily, contact is the right of the child. Certainly when a court considers an application for a contact order under CA89, the child's welfare is paramount, overriding the adults' interests.

However, adults must also be considered because everyone has a right to respect for their family life under the Human Rights Act 1998. But this right is not absolute and can be overridden in the interests of others, notably children who have their own rights – for example, not to be abused or mistreated (including emotionally). There is a balancing act to perform and, when rights are in conflict, children's rights prevail.

What is contact?

'Contact' goes beyond face-to-face meetings and includes all kinds of ways of maintaining links between children and people who are important to them.

DIRECT CONTACT

This means any face-to-face contact from a one-hour supervised visit once a month at a family centre to a two-week stay in summer.

Things to consider include:

- How frequent should meetings be?

- Where should visits take place – the foster home, a family centre, the family home or a neutral venue?

- How long should visits last? Too long can be as bad as too short – boredom can undermine the value of contact.

- What time of day should contact happen? If rehabilitation is planned, contact should be timed to allow the parent to undertake tasks like preparing meals or taking the child to school. Teenagers may resent contact after school if it stops them taking part in activities with their friends, or toddlers may be cranky if contact is when they normally have their nap.

- Should visits be supervised? If so, why and by whom? If as a foster carer you are asked to supervise contact, clarify exactly what your role is (see pp.130–131).

- Who should be present? Can the entire family turn up *en masse*? Should Dad be able to bring his new girlfriend?

- What extra arrangements are there for birthdays, school holidays, Christmas or other festivals, and how do these fit with the child's other activities at the same time (not least family life in the foster home)?

INDIRECT CONTACT

This can be as well as or instead of direct contact. At one extreme, contact may be limited to an annual information letter; in other cases regular and free communication is appropriate. Indirect contact includes all sorts of communication – letters, phone calls, emails, texts, cards and presents, photographs, videos and anything else you can think of. The exponential growth in electronic communications has greatly increased the options – and made contact more difficult to monitor: facilities like social networking sites can lead to unplanned, uncontrolled and sometimes unwanted contact.

Indirect contact arrangements need to be properly thought through – how often, who initiates the contact, is it one-way or two-way, what is the latest time for phone calls, are there limits to how many presents should be given and how elaborate or expensive they are – the list goes on.

As a foster carer, you are probably the best placed of all to think through the practical implications of a plan, and you should feel assertive enough to make sure arrangements are properly considered.

Supervising contact

It is important to understand why contact is supervised. What is supervision designed to prevent or to achieve? Is the supervisor there to monitor and record or to intervene? Is there a safety concern – if so, has a proper risk assessment been undertaken? Is the supervisor there to stop something inappropriate being said? Is every single interaction between adult and child to be observed and noted or just a general record kept? Is the supervisor there just to watch or actively to facilitate contact, suggesting activities, joining in and generally helping it go well? Is the supervisor to stay throughout or just to pop in occasionally? What is the supervisor to do if something inappropriate is said or done?

If you are asked to supervise contact, think carefully before agreeing. It is a skilled task and you should have specific training. Make sure you are absolutely clear about what the role entails in each case. Are you the right person to supervise contact for a child you are fostering? How would it affect your relationship with the child if, for example, you had to intervene between the child and the mother or if either of them saw you as spying on a private conversation? Are you too involved to be objective?

Careful notes must be taken of any supervised contact, remembering that these notes will be important in any review and could be used in court. You need to know whether you are expected to take detailed notes during contact or whether a summary written at the end of the visit is sufficient.

Notes should record the child's and parent's behaviour, reactions to the start and end of contact, activities during contact, any significant interactions, indications of the relationship and general mood of the visit, with anything significant said recorded, using exact words wherever possible.

If you are asked to have contact at your home, consider carefully whether this is right for the child and for you and your family (including other fostered children for whom arrangements might be different): you are not obliged to agree. Although you effectively work from home, it is still your home. You are as entitled as anyone else to respect for your home (guaranteed by the Human Rights Act 1998), to refuse entry to anyone and to ask anyone to leave.

Supervising phone calls and electronic communications poses particular practical difficulties and can feel very intrusive for the young person. If you are asked to do this, be very clear about the practical limitations and ensure that appropriate work is done so that the child understands the reasons for supervision and what you are being asked to do.

Does the child have to go to contact?

The legal obligations under CA89 are 'to allow' the child to have contact and to 'promote' contact. The law puts the emphasis on the child having contact with people, not the adults having contact with the child. The statutory wording makes it clear that the duty is to facilitate contact, not force it. Making a reluctant child go kicking and screaming to contact has nothing to do with CA89 and is no part of a foster carer's job. Of course, efforts should be made to find out why a child is reluctant to attend, and to encourage and facilitate contact where possible and appropriate.

Who is legally entitled to contact?
CHILDREN IN CARE
S34 CA89 deals with contact for children in care. S34(1) CA89 gives a presumption of 'reasonable contact' between the child and parents (with or without PR), guardians and anyone who had a residence order immediately before it was automatically discharged by the making of the care order. What is 'reasonable' is a matter for judgment by the local authority in all the circumstances.

REFUSING CONTACT
The court can make an order under s34(4) giving the local authority permission to refuse contact between a child in care and a named person who otherwise would be entitled to reasonable contact. This does not mean that contact is forbidden – it just gives the local authority the right to say no. A s34(4) order can be made at the same time as the care order or later on an application to court by either the local authority or the child.

If there is no s34(4) order but there is an urgent problem, the local authority can refuse contact for up to seven days provided this is necessary to safeguard or promote the child's welfare. Regulations set out the details of procedures and notifications. If seven days are not enough to resolve the problem, the local authority must go to court to seek a s34(4) order.

The court can make orders under s34(2) and (3) regulating contact between a named person and the child, perhaps specifying the nature or frequency of contact or imposing a supervision requirement. These orders can be made at the same time as the care order or later on application to court by the local authority, the person concerned or the child. So, if a child is really unhappy about contact arrangements, the child can apply to court, if necessary, for an order compelling or even terminating contact.

> Leon's parents Millie and Nathan are drug users and Nathan is violent. Leon lived with his aunt Olivia under a residence order, but she physically abused him. Borsetshire obtains a care order (automatically ending Olivia's residence order). Under s34(1), if no other orders are made, Millie, Nathan and Olivia all have a presumption of reasonable contact. Borsetshire must arrange contact that is appropriate in the circumstances, in consultation

with the adults, Leon and relevant professionals including Leon's foster mother Penny.

Borsetshire arranges supervised contact once a week for the parents and fortnightly for Olivia. Penny transports Leon to and from contact at the family centre, and carefully records Leon's comments and behaviour before and after contact. She feeds back regularly to her fostering officer and Leon's social worker. Her records and those of the contact supervisor are considered at Leon's reviews to see whether the contact remains appropriate and to make adjustments where necessary.

Nathan has become increasingly difficult. One day Penny is called to collect Leon early from contact because Nathan is being aggressive and threatening to staff and Leon is terrified. Borsetshire decides to issue an immediate suspension of contact. Things are not resolved in seven days, so Borsetshire applies to court for an order under s34(4) CA89 giving permission to refuse contact to Nathan. Leon's Children's Guardian and solicitor from the care proceedings are re-appointed to represent his interests, and all parties file evidence about the issue of contact. Penny's observations are important, and she writes a statement and gives evidence at court.

The court makes a s34(4) order so Borsetshire can refuse contact between Nathan and Leon. This does not mean that contact ends forever – in fact, the social worker works towards gradually re-introducing contact – but it does mean that Borsetshire has control including the power to say no to Nathan.

Accommodated children and contact

Most accommodated children have no involvement with the court at all. S34 CA89 only applies to children in care, not accommodated children. As accommodation is a purely voluntary arrangement, contact is a matter for negotiation and agreement between all concerned (including foster carers, of course). Deciding whom a child has contact with is part of PR, so legally speaking those who have PR (which does not include the local authority) have the final say. Sometimes arrangements can be flexible and informal, while in other cases it is better to draw up a clearer agreement, even though this is not legally binding.

Accommodated children may be subject to 'private law' orders made by the court in disputes between individuals. For example, separating parents may have been to court to resolve disputes about residence and contact under s8 CA89. These orders are not affected by a child being accommodated (whereas they would be automatically discharged by a care order), so they remain legally binding.

> Queenie's son Rob is accommodated in foster care under s20 CA89. Queenie's ex-partner Salvatore is not Rob's dad but was a father-figure to him. He does not have PR, but he has a contact order under s8 CA89 giving him contact once a fortnight. That order is unaffected by the fact that Rob is in foster care and it must be respected, even if Queenie (the only person with PR) hates Salvatore seeing Rob. Salvatore cannot discharge Rob from foster care because he has no PR, unless he goes back to court for a residence order under s8 CA89.

Contact for all looked after children

For all children who are looked after, whatever their legal status, the local authority must by law try to promote contact (unless it is not reasonably practicable or consistent with the child's welfare) between the child and his parents, others with PR and 'any relative, friend or other person connected with him'. This deliberately broad phrase is wide enough to include the child's whole family, even those the child may have lost touch with, such as relatives who are estranged from the parents. Grandparents can be particularly important figures for looked after children. The phrase also includes adults in the child's social circle who are not relatives – for example, parents' friends, a parent's former partner or former foster carers.

It is sometimes easy to focus so much on adults, especially parents (who may be very vocal in claiming their rights) that we overlook the child's relationships with other children. Siblings are often a vital connection, and where they are placed separately, contact should be a high priority. This may include siblings who remain at home, even if contact with the parents is limited or refused. And we must not forget unrelated children – friends might also be important and help to keep the child's life as 'normal' as possible.

As a foster carer, you probably know best who is really important to the child, especially those whom the child misses or would like to see less often, so you have a vital contribution to contact planning.

The child's rights

The child's wishes and feelings must be taken very seriously in decisions about contact. If care proceedings are ongoing, the Children's Guardian and solicitor must represent the child's views and ensure that his welfare is safeguarded. For all looked after children, the IRO must ensure that the care plan including contact meets the child's needs.

As the child's foster carer, you may need to help the child to contact the social worker, Guardian, solicitor and/or IRO, and also to express feelings.

If necessary, looked after children themselves may be able to apply to court for an order about contact, under s34 if they are in care or s8 if they are accommodated. They can do this themselves if they are of sufficient age and understanding to be competent, or an adult (possibly a foster carer) can take the case on their behalf.

Todd is 14 and in long-term foster care under a care order. He wants to see more of his mother and is desperate to see his sister, Unity, who is three and placed in a different foster home. His foster mum encourages him to talk to his IRO, who arranges an early review where Todd's wishes are considered and contact with his mum is increased; otherwise, the IRO would have taken up the issue with senior local authority officers and, if that was not successful, Todd, someone on his behalf or his mother could have made an application for a court order under s34.

However, the review cannot resolve Todd's contact with Unity because Unity's welfare must also be considered. Todd's social worker promises to talk to Unity's social worker. If contact cannot be agreed, Todd could apply to court. However, he would be the applicant and Unity would be the subject of the application. Her welfare, not Todd's, would be the court's paramount consideration. Even if it would be better for Todd to see Unity, the court will not order contact unless it is also the best thing for Unity.

Independent visitors

Some children lose contact with their families and have few visits or none at all. For such children, the local authority should appoint an independent visitor, a lay person to visit and befriend the child. Independent visitors are not social workers, substitute carers, professional advisers or counsellors, but they may have a role in contributing to children's welfare, boosting their self-esteem and encouraging them to exercise their rights and voice their opinions.

Points for practice

- Always be clear who has a legal right to contact with your fostered child and the effect of any court order.

- Make sure you have proper input into the contact plans for your fostered child, including practical considerations.

- Make sure your fostered child's voice is heard in contact arrangements.

- Be very clear about your role in contact.

- Do not agree to supervise contact unless you are sure it is appropriate, you have proper training and you are totally clear as to what the task entails.

Part III

Fostered Children and the Criminal Law

Chapter 11

The Criminal System – Some Legal Basics

Young people and criminal law

This section mainly concerns children over ten, so 'young person/people' are generally used instead of 'child/children'.

Some young people come into foster care via the criminal courts. Others become looked after through accommodation or care proceedings but later become involved in crime or disorder; unfortunately, looked after young people are more likely to be in trouble with the law than their counterparts.

Prevention

The first objective is to try to prevent young people from becoming involved in crime in the first place, or to reduce offending once they do. Diverting a young person from crime or anti-social behaviour can be an important aim of a care plan. Carers have an important role to play, providing positive role models, constructive experiences and sensible guidance.

At a strategic level, the Children Act 1989 (CA89) requires local authorities to encourage children not to commit criminal offences and to reduce the need for criminal proceedings. Under the Crime and Disorder Act 1998, authorities must produce an annual youth justice plan with a strategy and targets for reducing crime and disorder. The same Act makes preventing offending the principal aim of the whole youth justice system.

National initiatives include youth inclusion programmes in a number of deprived areas in England and Wales aiming to engage children from the age of eight who are at high risk of becoming involved in offending or anti-social behaviour. Early evaluation of the programmes showed promising results in reducing participants' offending.

The criminal justice system

Before considering details of the youth justice system, it is useful to understand some fundamentals.

Age of criminal responsibility

Children in England and Wales are criminally responsible for their actions, just like adults, from the age of ten, one of the lowest ages in Europe.

> Alistair has just turned ten. His friend Brett, who is a couple of weeks younger, is still nine. They attack and seriously injure another boy, both taking an equal part in the attack. Alistair can be arrested, charged and tried for a criminal offence such as assault occasioning grievous bodily harm. If he is found guilty, he will be punished.
>
> Brett, however, is too young to be prosecuted or punished, even if the boys are not caught until after Brett turns ten. However, this does not mean that nothing will be done, especially when the behaviour is so serious:
>
> - If his behaviour is a sign of significant harm, care proceedings could result.
>
> - He could be locked up in secure accommodation if a court makes an order under s25 CA89 on the basis that he may harm other people if he is kept in non-secure accommodation.
>
> - Alternatively, the local authority could apply to the FPC for a Child Safety Order (CSO) as he has done something that would have been a crime if he had been over ten. The order usually lasts for up to three months but in exceptional cases can last up to a year. Brett would be supervised by a social worker or a worker from the Youth Offending Team (YOT).

- Brett's parents could be made subject to a parenting order, requiring them to attend guidance or counselling for three months and comply for up to a year with conditions like attending school meetings, not letting Brett go unsupervised to particular places and making sure he is home by a certain time. Parenting orders can be made when a child is convicted of an offence, given an Anti-Social Behaviour Order (ASBO) or made subject to a CSO.

Purpose of the criminal law system

The criminal law defines and enforces society's norms. It sets the limits of acceptable behaviour – anyone straying beyond those limits commits a crime and is liable to prosecution and, if found guilty, punishment. Prosecutions are conducted in the Queen's name; cases are called, for example, '*R v Smith*', meaning the Queen against Smith. The Crown Prosecution Service (CPS) undertakes prosecutions, working closely with the police.

Purpose of the youth justice system

The Crime and Disorder Act 1998 made preventing youth offending the primary aim of the youth justice system. Courts also have a duty dating back to 1933 to 'have regard to the welfare' of a child or young person brought before the court. This is not as strong as the family court's duty to regard the child's welfare as 'paramount' but in youth justice the welfare of the defendant is a factor, which is not the case for adults.

What is YOT?

There is a YOT (sometimes called the Youth Offending Service – YOS) in every local authority area. These multi-agency teams include police, probation, children's social care, health, education, housing, and drug and alcohol services. YOT plays a crucial role in the whole youth justice process from preventative interventions through to re-settling young offenders into the community following a custodial sentence. They provide assessments, court reports and intervention programmes.

If you foster a young person who is or may be involved in offending, a good working relationship with your local YOT is invaluable.

What is a crime?

In our system there is no single criminal code listing all criminal offences. This makes it difficult to find out exactly what is and is not illegal. Offences are found in literally hundreds of statutes. Some, like the Theft Act 1968, obviously deal with crime, but offences are also tucked away in unexpected places like CA89. Some offences (notably murder) are not statutory but have come down through decided cases over the centuries (known as 'common law').

Offences usually consist of a number of detailed elements and, to secure a conviction, the prosecution must prove each part of the defined offence, often including a mental element – intention (acting on purpose), recklessness (taking an unjustified risk) or negligence (doing something a reasonable person would not do). Some offences are 'strict liability' – a crime is committed just by doing the act, regardless of fault.

> Steve is accused of stealing a sports holdall. The legal definition of theft is that someone 'dishonestly appropriates property belonging to another with the intention of permanently depriving the other of it'. For Steve to be convicted of theft, the prosecution must prove that:
>
> - Steve acted dishonestly
> - he took something belonging to someone else, and
> - he intended to treat it as his own, keeping it or selling it on.
>
> Steve's defence is that the holdall looked just like one he owns himself. He picked it up by mistake. He was stopped by the police when he was on his way back to the sports centre to hand it in. If Steve is telling the truth, it is not theft: he took someone else's property, but by mistake; he did not have the necessary intention to make his action criminal.

Key principles

Presumption of innocence

Everyone is innocent until proven guilty. This is guaranteed under the European Convention on Human Rights and the Human Rights Act 1998.

Burden of proof

The prosecution must prove its case; it is not for the defendant to prove innocence. The defendant is asked to plead 'guilty' or 'not guilty' – not 'guilty' or 'innocent'. Someone who knows he is guilty can legitimately plead 'not guilty', challenging the prosecution to prove its case. If it fails to do so, the defendant walks free.

The verdict at the end of a trial is 'guilty' or 'not guilty'. 'Not guilty' might mean that the court believed the defendant was innocent or thought the defendant was probably guilty but could not be sure enough. We will never know – unlike family courts, which give reasons for their decisions, criminal courts just announce a verdict. No-one, not even the judge, knows what is discussed in the jury room.

Standard of proof

How sure does the court have to be to reach a decision? In a criminal trial the prosecution must prove the case 'beyond reasonable doubt', as sure as it is realistically possible to be.

This is very different from the standard in family cases where the standard of proof is 'on the balance of probabilities', meaning 'more likely than not'.

> Fourteen-year-old Connie alleges sexual abuse by her father David. Two court cases follow: care proceedings are taken to protect Connie, and David is prosecuted for indecent assault.
>
> The care proceedings take place in the County Court. The local authority is the applicant and David, Connie and Connie's mother are respondents.
>
> The criminal trial takes place in the Crown Court. The Crown prosecutes David who is the defendant. Connie is merely a witness in the case.
>
> The evidence shows that David probably sexually abused Connie. This is enough for care proceedings – the local authority has to prove its case on the balance of probabilities. The judge makes a finding that David sexually abused Connie and makes a care order.
>
> In the criminal case it is a different matter. 'He probably did it' is not enough for a finding of guilt. The jury must acquit David.
>
> Connie needs her carer's help to understand how one court apparently believed her while the other, as it seems to her, did not and that David will walk free, an innocent man.

Right to a fair trial

This right (Article 6 of the European Convention on Human Rights) is enshrined in the Human Rights Act 1998. Everyone has the right to 'a fair and public hearing within a reasonable time by an independent and impartial tribunal established by law', although the element of publicity is usually limited to protect young defendants.

It also guarantees safeguards to ensure that the defendant understands the case against him. Everyone charged with a criminal offence has the right to:

- be informed promptly in a language they understand (a spoken or signed language, or simply age-appropriate language) the detail of the accusation against them

- have an interpreter in court if they need it

- legal advice

- adequate time and facilities to prepare their defence

- cross-examine prosecution witnesses

- call witnesses in their defence.

In 1993, Robert Thompson and Jon Venables, aged ten, murdered two-year-old Jamie Bulger. They were tried over the course of three weeks in the Crown Court under the glare of hostile publicity. In 1999, they applied to the European Court of Human Rights, which found that the trial had breached the boys' right to a fair trial because:

> it was highly unlikely that the applicant would have felt sufficiently uninhibited, in the tense court room and under public scrutiny, to have consulted with [his lawyers] during the trial or, indeed, that, given his immaturity and his disturbed emotional state, he would have been capable outside the court room of co-operating with his lawyers and giving them information for the purpose of his defence.[1]

---

1   *V v UK* Application no, 24888/94; judgment 16.12.99 paragraph 90.

Right to remain silent

As it is up to the prosecution to prove its case, the defendant is under no obligation to help by answering questions. When someone is arrested, before police interview and again before charge, the person must be given the caution: 'You do not have to say anything. But it may harm your defence if you do not mention when questioned something which you later rely on in court. Anything you do say may be given in evidence.' There is an equivalent formula in Welsh.

> Evan is arrested for burglary. He remains silent in interview. At trial he produces an alibi, bringing friends as witnesses claiming that he was with them on the night in question. The jury is entitled to 'draw an adverse inference'; they are entitled to think 'if this was really true, he would have said so straight away', unless there is another plausible reason for not doing so – perhaps Evan was under a curfew from a previous offence and knew that he shouldn't have been out at the time.
>
> The 'adverse inference' on its own cannot prove the case beyond reasonable doubt – the prosecution must still produce positive evidence of Evan's guilt – but the jury can take their scepticism about the alibi into account when deciding their verdict.

Criminal courts

The Youth Court is a special division of the Magistrates' Court hearing criminal cases against 10–17-year-olds. If a defendant turns 18 part-way through a case, the Youth Court can finish it or transfer it to the adult Magistrates' Court. However, the Youth Court cannot deal with a new charge once a defendant has turned 18.

Very serious cases (such as murder, manslaughter or serious sexual or violent crimes) involving defendants of any age, even ten-year-olds, are heard by judge and jury in the Crown Court.

If a young person is charged jointly with an adult, the case against both may be heard in an adult court. This is more likely if, for example, the two defendants are 17 and 18 than if they are 45 and 12.

Even if the trial takes place in the Youth Court, a young person who is a 'dangerous offender' and convicted of a violent or sexual offence can be sent for sentencing to the Crown Court, where tougher penalties are available.

Adult Magistrates' Courts and Crown Courts are open to the public. Go as an observer to see how they work, rather than to find yourself entering a court for the first time supporting a young defendant. Youth Courts are not open to the public, but magistrates may allow a carer to observe for training purposes – ask your fostering officer if this can be arranged.

Lay involvement in decisions

Most magistrates are lay people with no legal qualifications and in the Crown Court the verdict is decided by a jury of 12 ordinary citizens.

Strict rules of evidence

Getting a criminal record is a serious matter, and a conviction might lead to someone losing their liberty. Therefore, there are very strict rules and safeguards about what evidence is allowed and how it must be obtained.

> Francis is interviewed by the police, but they forget to caution him first. He confesses to the crime. But because his rights have not been explained to him, his confession is inadmissible in court. The jury will never know that Francis confessed.

The rules of evidence are much stricter in criminal courts than in family courts, which can consider a much wider range of information. Hearsay (second-hand) evidence is not admissible in criminal courts where witnesses have to speak for themselves, but it is allowed in children's cases in the family court, because the focus is on the child's welfare, not guilt or innocence.

> George, aged eight, tells his carer Helen that his mother beat him with a belt. In George's care proceedings, Helen can make a statement and give evidence in court on George's behalf about what he said. In the criminal case against George's mother, Helen cannot speak for George – he has to give his own evidence.[2]

---

2   For more information on children giving evidence in court, see Chapter 16.

Interaction of criminal and family cases

Sometimes the same situation gives rise to two different court cases, one family and one criminal, as in Connie's case (discussed earlier). Alternatively, the young person could be at the centre of both cases.

> Idris is 14. He is excluded from school, funds his drug habit by stealing and is involved in violence. His family life is chaotic.
>
> The children and families team see his case as one of child protection – he is suffering significant harm through inadequate parenting or being beyond control – and they take care proceedings. The police see his behaviour as criminal when he is arrested for a serious assault and prosecuted.
>
> The care case takes place in the Family Proceedings Court (FPC) or County Court. It looks at significant harm and Idris's welfare, considering all his circumstances, relationships and needs. The evidence is wide-ranging under flexible rules. Idris has a Children's Guardian and a solicitor. His parents are respondents. The court decides the case on the balance of probabilities.
>
> The criminal case takes place in the Youth Court or Crown Court. It looks at the precise offences Idris is charged with, judging whether the prosecution has proven the case beyond reasonable doubt. Only the prosecution and Idris as defendant are involved. Idris is represented by a lawyer. The court only concerns itself about aspects of Idris's life other than the offences if he is convicted and it needs to consider what sentence to impose.

Points for practice

- Understanding the key elements of the criminal justice system means you can help a young person involved in the system.

- Make sure you understand the relationship between the criminal system and the family system, and can explain it to a young person involved in both.

- Find out where your local Magistrates', Youth and Crown Courts are. If you are unfamiliar with courts, go along as an observer.

- If you foster a young person who is or may become involved in the youth justice system, make contact with your local YOT and community police team. Seek training.

Chapter 12

The Criminal Process

Police powers

Stop and search

The police have the power to stop people on the street and ask them where they are going and what they have been doing.[1] They may search people – asking them to turn out their pockets or bag and remove outer clothing – or a vehicle. The police must identify themselves (name and number) and the reasons for the stop. The people concerned are temporarily detained for the duration of the stop, and the police can use reasonable force they do not co-operate.

'Stop and search' is justified to prevent terrorism or if the officer has reasonable suspicion that the person is in possession of:

- stolen goods
- an offensive weapon
- tools to commit a burglary or other crime
- controlled drugs.

The police may not stop and search people just because of their:

- age
- gender
- race
- religion

1   For full details of police stop and search powers and how they should be exercised, see PACE Code A. Available at www.homeoffice.gov.uk/police/powers/pace-codes, accessed on 6 July 2010.

- other personal characteristic, such as sexual orientation or disability

- style of dress

- previous criminal record.

Stop and search

There has been a burglary by a tall, slim young black man wearing dark clothing. Shortly afterwards, a policeman sees a man fitting that description, walking quickly and looking nervous. The officer has reason to suspect that he might be the burglar, and can stop and search him. This is a lawful search.

Another police officer sees a group of young black men hanging around in a shopping centre. They are not doing anything in particular, although shoppers are giving them a wide berth. The officer thinks they look like troublemakers, so decides to stop and search them. This is not a lawful stop – there are no reasonable grounds for suspicion.

A third officer hears of the burglary. He thinks he can guess who did it. Later he sees the man he has in mind and stops for an informal chat. He does not carry out a formal stop and search knowing this would be unlawful, based solely on the man's past record.

If the police find nothing and have no reason to arrest, they complete a form and give a copy to the person concerned, who is then free to go. This gives details of the reasons for the stop and search, its outcome and the officer's name. The form notes the person's ethnic origin to allow monitoring in order to ensure the power is not misused.

If you or a fostered young person are stopped and searched unreasonably or not treated with respect, you can complain to your local police station, the Independent Police Complaints Commission or the Equality and Human Rights Commission.

Can the police search your home?

The right to respect for your home is enshrined in the Human Rights Act 1998. Normally, you can invite anyone into your home (including the police), refuse entry to anyone or ask someone to leave once they have entered. The police can only enter your home against your will and by force if necessary if they have:

- a search warrant issued by a magistrate (perhaps to search for stolen property or drugs, or for evidence of a serious offence), or

- a statutory power to make an arrest or following an arrest.

Powers to search premises also bring the power to seize relevant property including anything specified in a warrant and any evidence of crime. Electronic equipment like computers and mobile phones might be seized for forensic examination.

The police should always explain their legal authority for a search, act courteously and respectfully, and only use reasonable force if absolutely necessary. Searches should be carried out at a reasonable time of day unless that would defeat the object. The search must only be such as is necessary to achieve its objective – a search for small packets of heroin might justify rifling through drawers, whereas a search for stolen TVs would not. The search must end when its objective is achieved – for example, when everything specified in the warrant has been found. The premises must be left secure.

After a search, the police must give you a notice specifying the legal authority for the search and your rights.[2]

Arrest

Not all criminal cases start with an arrest; some more minor cases start with a charge sent by post. The police can arrest someone if:

- they cannot ascertain the person's name and address or believe the details given are false

- arrest is necessary to protect a child or other vulnerable person

- arrest is necessary to stop the person:

  ○ injuring himself or others

  ○ causing loss or damage to property

  ○ committing an offence against public decency

  ○ obstructing the highway.

---

2   For full details of police search and seizure powers, see PACE Code B. Available at www.homeoffice.gov.uk/police/powers/pace-codes, accessed on 6 July 2010.

Some people other than the police, such as store detectives and transport police, also have arrest powers.

Being arrested simply means that people are not free to go – they do not necessarily have to be handcuffed or forcibly restrained. The suspects should be cautioned on arrest and are then usually taken straight to the police station. Alternatively, the police officer can bail the suspects, requiring them to go to the station on a specified date.

Going to the police station voluntarily

No-one is obliged to go to the station 'to help with enquiries'. It is quite simple: if you are not under arrest, you can refuse to go to the station or, if you do go, you can leave at any time.

Time limits for detention without charge

The clock only starts to run when someone is under arrest, so time spent voluntarily at the police station does not count. Suspects cannot usually be held without charge for more than 36 hours, although for young people that is reduced 24 hours unless they are suspected of a serious crime and bail is inappropriate. The Magistrates' Court can extend time limits in serious cases.

Detention at the police station is only to allow the police to decide whether or not to charge the suspect with an offence. It is not to punish the suspect or to protect the public.

The custody officer (who is not involved in the investigation) must regularly review the detention to ensure it remains justified.

Detention ends when the suspect is:

- charged

- given a reprimand or warning

- released without charge, or

- released on bail to report to the station at a later date, if enquiries are not yet completed.

Rights at the police station

LEGAL ADVICE

Everyone attending the police station voluntarily or under arrest must be told of their right to free legal advice before questioning and during interview. They are entitled to speak privately with their solicitor and anything said between them remains confidential.

INFORMING SOMEONE OF THE ARREST

The police must contact one person likely to be interested in the suspect's welfare (such as a foster carer). If that person is not contactable, up to two others may be tried. Suspects are also entitled to make one phone call each unless there are exceptional circumstances (e.g. if they might tip someone off to destroy evidence).

RIGHT TO CONSULT THE POLICE AND CRIMINAL EVIDENCE (PACE) CODES OF PRACTICE

The Police and Criminal Evidence Act 1984 (known as PACE) is the key statute covering police powers, procedures and safeguards in criminal investigations. Codes of Practice are issued under PACE and regularly updated. They are not strictly legally binding but any evidence obtained contrary to the Codes is likely to be inadmissible in court.

The Codes are long and not particularly user-friendly, but they do set out in detail a suspect's rights and police duties so, if you attend the station with a young person, ask to see a copy and check that proper procedures are followed. Better still, look them up in advance and try to get to grips with their main provisions.

CONTACTING A PARENT OR GUARDIAN

The custody officer must contact a parent, guardian or the local authority (if the young suspect is looked after) to inform them of the arrest, the reasons for it and where the young person is being held. This is as well as the right to have someone informed of the arrest.

CUSTODY RECORD

This is established as soon as a suspect arrives at the station, and it records every action and decision taken while the person is there. The suspect has a right to a copy.

Investigating criminal offences

QUESTIONING SUSPECTS

The interview is a key weapon in the police armoury; most criminals are convicted because of what they say in police interview. The appropriate adult (AA) has an important role in police interview for a young suspect (for more details see pp.157–158). Interviewing must stop as soon as there is enough evidence to charge the suspect, and there is generally no further interviewing after charge.

SEARCHES

The detainee may be searched, but this is usually limited to removing outer clothing. Detailed rules (in Annex A of Code C)[3] apply if a strip search or intimate search is needed. Searches must be carried out by an officer of the same sex as the detainee and the AA must be present. If clothing has to be retained for investigation such as DNA testing or simply for hygienic reasons, suitable clean replacements must be provided.

DRUG TESTING

Suspects who are 14 or over and arrested for certain offences can be required to provide a sample for drug testing – there are detailed provisions in Code C.

INTERVIEWING WITNESSES

As well as interviewing the suspect, the police also interview anyone else with relevant information about the offence, possibly including you as the young person's carer. The duty to help the police investigate crimes is a civic one, not a legal one, and no-one can be forced to give a statement to the police. However, if you do so, you can be called to give evidence by either the prosecution or the defence and, if necessary, your attendance can be compelled by a witness summons; it is contempt of court (potentially punishable by imprisonment) not to comply.

Witness statements to the police are usually recorded in writing by the police officer on a standard form, which you are then asked to sign. Read it very carefully and never sign unless you are happy with every

---

3   PACE Code C available at www.homeoffice.gov.uk/police/powers/pace-codes, accessed on 6 July 2010.

word of the statement. If the case goes to court, your statement will form part of the prosecution papers copied to the defence.

IDENTIFICATION

There are detailed procedures for identification parades, video or group identification, taking fingerprints, taking samples (non-intimate samples like hair or saliva or intimate samples like blood or semen) and carrying out DNA testing.[4] Procedures must be explained to the young person in the AA's presence. Some identification procedures require a parent's consent (the local authority's if the person is in care) as well as the young person's. Fingerprints can, however, be taken without consent. All the details are in PACE Code D.

AA

As a foster carer, you may be asked to act as the young person's AA. This a key role, described fully in PACE Code C and is designed to protect the interests of young or vulnerable suspects.

Who gets an AA?

Anyone who is or appears to be aged under 17 or mentally ill or disabled must have an AA. Seventeen-year-olds who are not otherwise vulnerable are not entitled to an AA. They are treated as if they were adults at the police station even though, if charged, their cases still go to the Youth Court.

Who is 'appropriate'?

AAs must be over 18. Code C says that an AA is one of the following.

- A parent or guardian.

- A local authority representative for a looked after child.

- A social worker.

- Failing the above, any other responsible adult.

---

4   PACE Code D. Available at www.homeoffice.gov.uk/police/powers/pace-codes, accessed 6 July 2010.

Who is not appropriate?

- A police officer or employee.

- Anyone involved in the alleged offence.

- A victim of or witness to the alleged offence.

- Anyone to whom the suspect has confessed (but don't give this as your reason for refusing to act!).

- A parent who is estranged from the child, but only if the child objects.

- An interpreter, solicitor or independent custody visitor – each person can only fulfil one role at a time.

The law does not require an AA to have any particular training or knowledge – in fact most AAs are simply the young person's parent. Many AAs are thought to be ineffective, either remaining passive or becoming too partisan.

Must I act as AA?

No-one is obliged to act as an AA. Check your agency's policies and procedures. Consider carefully the implications for your relationship with the young person and role as carer if you either agree or refuse. If in doubt, seek advice.

If you agree to act, you should be told where the young person is and the grounds for the detention. The custody officer will ask you to come to the police station and of course you should do so urgently.

What should an AA do?
FIRST STEPS

- Stay calm – be confident and composed at all times.

- Take a notepad and pen. Note down names and numbers of all police officers involved.

- Note the time at every stage and monitor time limits.

- Ask to see the custody record. Ask for an explanation of anything in it you are uncertain or unhappy about.

- Find out what offence is suspected, who is involved, whether the young person is under arrest or there voluntarily, and whether the young person has said anything about the alleged offence.

- If your young person needs an interpreter (for a spoken or signed language), insist on one being provided immediately – they are provided without charge.

- Ask for a copy of Code C and refer to it throughout.

YOUNG SUSPECTS' RIGHTS

- Suspects should already have been told of their rights (to have someone informed of their arrest, to have legal advice and to see the Codes) but this must be repeated in an AA's presence.

- The suspects should be told that the AA is there to advise and assist them and they can speak privately at any time. Always insist on talking in private – conversations that are overheard could be used in evidence.

- The caution must be repeated in the AA's presence. Make sure the young person understands what it means, explaining it in your own words if that helps.

- Check the detailed rules in the PACE Codes if the police propose to carry out searches or take samples.

GET A LAWYER

All suspects are entitled to legal advice and a duty solicitor is always available. Even if your foster children do not want a lawyer, insist on one attending – as AA, you can and should override their refusal. You cannot make them co-operate with the lawyer when the lawyer arrives, but at least you will have ensured that they have the option.

Don't sit in on the consultation between the lawyer and the young person – lawyers cannot be questioned about what is said in a legal consultation; AAs can.

CHECK AND MONITOR CUSTODY CONDITIONS

Code C contains details about custody conditions for young people.

- They should not be in a cell unless there is no other secure accommodation available and they cannot be supervised otherwise – if your young person is in a cell, find out why, note the answer and check the custody record.

- If a suspect must be in a cell, there should be no further restraints unless absolutely necessary.

- A young suspect should never be in a cell with an adult.

- Accommodation for suspects should be clean, adequately warm and adequately lit.

- Suspects are entitled to:

  ○ refreshments (one main meal and two light meals a day, with drinks at reasonable intervals), respecting specific dietary needs and religious beliefs. Be sure to inform the police of any special requirements

  ○ rest (8 hours every 24 hours, usually at night)

  ○ medical attention – ask for a doctor if you think your young person is mentally or physically ill, drunk or under the influence of drugs, or has a medical condition (especially one that requires regular medication).

- Detained suspects should be visited at least every hour. If they seem drunk or under the influence of drugs, they should be visited at least every half hour and roused if asleep, to ensure they are not unconscious.

If you are unhappy about any aspect of your young person's treatment, complain to a senior officer.

IN POLICE INTERVIEW

- Unless circumstances are exceptional, young suspects must not be interviewed without an AA and a lawyer (if requested).

- Interviews at the police station are tape-recorded. At the start of the interview all those present (including the AA) must identify themselves.

- The police should tell you that, as AA, your role is not just to observe but to advise the suspect, observe whether the interview is conducted properly and fairly, and aid communication.

- Make a note of the time the interview starts, when it ends and any breaks.

- Make sure suspects understand the questions put to them and that the police understand their answers. This is particularly important if they have learning or communication difficulties, or are distressed.

- Be prepared to step in – to explain what is being said, to ask for a break or to stop intimidation or bullying – even if the solicitor does not.

- You can talk to the young person in private at any time – even after the interview has started.

- If a statement is written down during the interview, you should read and sign it. Only sign if it accurately reflects what the young suspect said.

- There should be breaks during the interview at normal meal-times and short breaks at least every two hours.

Spot the mistakes

Gemma, aged 14, is arrested for burglary. The police call her foster father Henry as AA. Henry says he is not surprised to be called as Gemma is in with a bad crowd, stays out late and brings home games consoles, ipods and so on, claiming her mother gave them to her. Henry asks the custody officer for a copy of Code D. The police tell Henry they must repeat the caution in his presence, but he says not to worry as he's sure they have done it already. Then he goes to see Gemma in the cell, where a man is asleep on the other bed. The cell smells strongly of urine and vomit. Gemma seems drowsy and unwell. Henry asks to speak to Gemma outside the cell, so as not to disturb the sleeping man, and talks to her in the corridor. Gemma says she just wants to go home. Henry suggests that, in that case, she should not wait for the solicitor – all she has to do is tell the truth. He reminds her how they have been working on being honest and taking responsibility for behaviour. Gemma agrees to go ahead with the interview although she seems half-asleep. Part-way through she asks for a break. The police officer loses his temper and shouts at Gemma, telling her to stop playing for time and calling her a thieving slut. Henry tells Gemma he is not surprised that people get cross with her and urges her to own up to what she has done. Gemma says, 'Okay, I did it – can I go home now?' Henry praises her for her honesty.

Comments

- Henry started by making prejudicial comments about Gemma, including information which could be used against her.

- Henry asked for the wrong Code – it should be Code C.

- An AA should always insist on procedures being followed – Henry is wrong to tell the police not to repeat the caution.

- Henry should challenge why Gemma is in a cell at all. She should certainly not be in a cell with an adult male. The cell conditions breach Code C.

- Henry fails to seek medical attention for Gemma and seems more concerned about the male detainee.

- Henry should speak to Gemma in private, not in a corridor. An AA should never discourage a young suspect from having a solicitor – on the contrary, AAs should insist on seeking a lawyer.

- Henry blurs his boundaries – as a foster carer he may be working with Gemma on honesty but as an AA his job is to safeguard her rights as a suspect.

- The police interview should not proceed without a lawyer and not when Gemma is sleepy. Gemma is entitled to a break and it should be Henry who asks for it.

Not only does Henry fail to intervene to stop the policeman's inappropriate behaviour and language, he actually reinforces it. Henry is wrong to encourage Gemma in the police interview to confess and wrong to praise her for doing so, especially when it seems her motivation is simply to go home. Throughout, Henry appears to collude with the police rather than protecting Gemma's rights and ensuring that proper procedures are followed.

Points for practice

- Be aware of your rights and those of the young people you foster.

- Know your agency's policies and procedures on carers acting as AAs.

- If you are likely to act as an AA:

  - get to grips with Code C in advance

  - seek training.

Chapter 13

Reprimands, Warnings and Court

Reprimand, warning or charge

Once the police believe there is enough evidence for a realistic prospect of conviction, there are three options:

1. Reprimand.

2. Warning.

3. Charge.

The police can give a young person bail for a YOT assessment to be carried out before deciding which route to take.

Reprimands and warnings

Eleven-year-old Keanu is caught red-handed shoplifting. He has never been in trouble before, and only stole a small amount. He is full of remorse and immediately admits his guilt. He could be charged and prosecuted, but that may not be necessary and it would suck him into the criminal system – a formal telling-off might steer him away from further offending. A reprimand is the ideal solution.

Reprimands

To be eligible for a reprimand, an offender must:

- be between 10 and 17

- be a first-time offender

- admit guilt of a crime that is not grave.

There must be enough evidence for a charge and prosecution – this is not a way for the police to avoid a weak case going to court – but prosecution is not in the public interest.

The reprimand can be given immediately, or the young person can be bailed to come back later to be reprimanded. The reprimand is given orally in the AA's presence and backed up in writing.

> Keanu goes to the police station with his foster dad as AA. A senior officer in uniform delivers the reprimand. It is very formal. The officer reminds Keanu of the offence he committed for which he is being reprimanded. He makes it clear that this is a serious matter – Keanu is in no way being 'let off' and this reprimand will stay on his record until he is 18. He tells him that, if he gets in trouble again, he will get a final warning or will be taken to court. If he is convicted, this reprimand will be taken into account in sentencing.
>
> Keanu's details are passed to the YOT who do not have to intervene but may do so, particularly if they feel that Keanu is at high risk of further offending.

Final warnings

> Keanu has been arrested again along with three friends, Leo, Mohamed and Nuala, for throwing stones causing relatively minor criminal damage. There is clear evidence that all four were involved. The three boys admit the offence and express remorse. Nuala says it was only the boys who threw stones, not her. Mohamed and Nuala have never been in trouble with the police before. Keanu has had a reprimand and Leo has a previous conviction. Although all four were involved in the same incident, the outcomes may be different. Nuala denies the offence. Reprimands and warnings are only available if the offender admits guilt so, even though this is her first involvement with the police, there are only two options – charge or let the matter drop, depending on the public interest.
>
> Mohamed is a first-time offender who admits the offence. He is eligible for a reprimand.
>
> Keanu has already had a reprimand and cannot have another one. As he has no convictions, a final warning is an option, instead of proceeding to charge.

> Leo has a conviction, so he is not eligible for a reprimand or warning. Like Nuala, the only two choices for him are charge or no action.

Warnings do not always follow reprimands – they can be given for first offences that are too serious for a reprimand but not serious enough for a charge. They are one stage up from reprimands, and involve an automatic referral to the YOT for assessment and the devising of a programme to divert from further offending. Participation in the YOT programme is voluntary, but failure to co-operate will come back to haunt the young people should they later be convicted of another offence.

Many YOT programmes for final warnings include an element of restorative justice (making offenders face up to and take responsibility for their crimes, and make reparation) and victims may also be involved if they want to be.

A final warning is usually a very last chance to avoid prosecution. Occasionally, a second warning may be given, if at least two years have passed since the first, but generally any further offending after a warning lands the young person in court.

Implications of reprimands and warnings

Reprimands and warnings are not convictions, and they are 'spent' as soon as they are issued so they do not need to be mentioned in job applications. But they are not without consequences. They remain on police records until the young person is 18 or for 5 years (whichever is longer). They may still show up on enhanced CRB disclosures and remain relevant for employment with children and vulnerable adults where even 'spent' offences count. Reprimands and warnings for relevant sexual offences lead to entry on the sex offenders register. And if the young person later comes up for sentencing in court, previous reprimands and warnings will be taken into account, possibly leading to a tougher sentence.

Charge

Other than dropping the matter altogether, a charge is the only option if the young person:

- has a previous conviction, or

- has had a final warning within the last two years, or

- has had two final warnings (however long ago), or

- is suspected of an offence (even a first offence) serious enough to warrant proceeding straight to a charge, or

- denies the offence.

The police decide whether to charge and may consult the CPS before doing so. Once the charge is laid, the CPS takes over the prosecution, keeping it under constant review.

Before charge and in an AA's presence, the young people are cautioned again. They are then told that they are charged with a specified offence, giving both the technical details of the offence (which section of which Act applies) and a plain English version. They receive a written notice recording the same information.

After charge

Before trial, a defendant's liberty should be restricted no more than necessary. So the starting point is bail not remand, and unconditional rather than conditional bail. Most young people go home from the police station on bail with a date to go to court.

Bail

Bail means release between leaving the station and the first court date, or between one court hearing and the next. It can be unconditional (except for the obligation to go to court) or on conditions that are necessary to:

- ensure the defendants attend court

- stop them offending while on bail

- stop them interfering with witnesses or otherwise obstructing justice

- ensure they attend appointments – for example, for reports or enquiries.

Conditions can range from reporting to the police station on particular days to living at a certain address, staying away from specified places, being supervised by the YOT on a bail support and supervision programme, or electronic tagging (for over 12-year-olds). A notice sets out in clear terms exactly what the defendant must or must not do.

If you are caring for young peole on bail, make sure that they understand any conditions and stick to them. Breaching bail conditions is a criminal offence in itself and will only get the young person into further trouble.

Refusing bail

Bail can be refused if there are good grounds to believe that, even with bail conditions:

- the defendants will not come to court

- the defendants will commit further offences on bail

- the defendants will interfere with witnesses or

- it is not in the defendants' own interests (e.g. because they would be better off in foster care).

If bail is refused, the defendant is remanded.

Remand

Remand is some form of detention pending trial. Seventeen-year-old defendants are treated as adults, so for them remand means custody in a remand centre or young offenders' institution (YOI).

For 12–16-year-olds, remand is usually to local authority accommodation. A remanded young person becomes a looked after child. Normally, the local authority decides where to place young people unless the court specifies otherwise, such as ordering that they should not be placed at home with their parents. Other conditions can be attached, just as for young people on bail.

Remand to local authority accommodation often means foster care, ideally in a specialist remand foster placement where the carers have training, support and close links to the YOT. Carers need to be very clear about their roles, boundaries and procedures, like when and how to report a young person who goes missing or breaks a curfew. Remand fostering may make a custodial sentence less likely on conviction and research shows that it can reduce re-offending.[1]

SECURE REMANDS

However, sometimes remand to the local authority, even with stringent conditions, is not enough. If young people aged between 12 and 16 are accused of a really serious crime and it is necessary to protect the public from serious harm or to stop further serious offending, the court can order them to be locked up by remanding them with a 'security requirement'. Girls aged 12–16 and boys aged 12–14 (or 14–16 if they are vulnerable) are placed in secure accommodation. Fifteen- and 16-year-old boys go to a remand centre.

HOW LONG DOES REMAND LAST?

If the police refuse bail, the young person must be brought before the court without delay. If the court refuses bail, the first remand is for a maximum of 8 days and after that for up to 28 days at a time. This means that the case is regularly reviewed. Courts aim to proceed to full trial as soon as possible and to keep the number of remands to a minimum.

ELECTRONIC TAGGING

Tagging is a form of surveillance, particularly used to monitor curfews, via a base station connected to a phone line at the person's home or using GPS satellite technology and a tag securely attached to the young person's ankle. If the tag is not within range or is disconnected or otherwise not working, the tagging company alerts the authorities to follow the matter up to see if there has been a breach.

Going to court

Courts try to deal quickly with young people's cases in order to keep a clear connection between the offence and its consequences. At the first hearing young people are asked whether they plead guilty or not guilty. If they plead guilty, there is no need for a full trial and the court can

---

1   See the Nacro *Youth Crime Briefing: Remand Fostering* (2004). Available at www.baaf. org.uk/info/remandfost.pdf, accessed on 6 July 2010.

go straight on to sentencing.[2] If they plead not guilty, the court sets a timetable and issues directions to get everything ready for trial as soon as possible.

In between court hearings, the young defendants will have to meet their lawyer to go through the evidence and prepare their case. Make sure your young people attend these meetings and co-operate fully with their lawyer, who is on their side and the only person in the whole process who keeps absolutely confidential whatever the client says.

Youth Courts

Thirteen-year-old Dean has to go to the Youth Court. His foster mother Ellie goes too – in fact for defendants under 16 a parent or parent-figure must attend court and could be arrested if they fail to do so. Dean and Ellie have little idea of what to expect – their only image of court is from TV so they feel rather intimidated. Ellie persuades Dean to dress smartly in his school uniform. They arrive in plenty of time for the hearing.

The Youth Court is held in the same building as the Magistrates' Court, but in a separate area so Dean and Ellie don't have to mix with adult defendants. The usher takes their names and shows them where to wait and which court the case will be in. Dean's solicitor arrives and sees him in a private interview room. She specialises in youth crime and explains things clearly without talking down to Dean.

Once they get into court, Ellie is surprised that everyone sits at the same level – she expected to see the magistrates sitting on high. Dean sits with Ellie on one side for support and his solicitor on the other, so he can communicate easily with her throughout the hearing. Everyone stands when the magistrates come in, and Dean has to stand when they are talking to him, but for most of the time everyone is sitting down.

The magistrate in the middle explains that she is the Chair and introduces everyone in the courtroom – the other magistrates, their legal adviser, the usher, the CPS lawyer prosecuting the case and the YOT worker. She explains what will happen. She addresses Dean by his first name, uses plain language and looks him straight in the eye. She often checks that Dean understands what is going on and encourages him to speak up for himself. Ellie is surprised that sometimes the Chair talks to her and asks what she thinks. The

---

2   For more details on sentencing, see Chapter 14.

whole procedure is less intimidating than Dean and Ellie expected, although Dean is still in no doubt that this is a serious matter.

SPECIAL NEEDS

Arrangements can be made to help defendants according to their needs – for example, interpreters or signers are available, seating arrangements in court can be changed to facilitate lip-reading, or documents can be read out loud for a defendant with literacy problems. Some older court buildings are still not easily accessible to people with disabilities, so a case might be transferred to another more modern court with better facilities. As the carer, you probably know better than anyone what assistance the young person needs to be able to participate fully. Flag up any special considerations early on.

Trials

Criminal trials follow the same basic outline as contested hearings in the family courts.

Dean pleads not guilty. The trial might last for some time so the Chair makes sure that there are regular breaks.

The CPS lawyer opens the prosecution case against Dean, explaining what he intends to prove. He then calls his witnesses one by one. Each takes the oath or affirms, and then gives evidence. Unlike the family court, criminal courts do not read the witness statements, so the CPS lawyer asks them non-leading questions taking them through their evidence. Dean's solicitor then cross-examines them. She is vigorous and challenging, trying to show up inconsistencies, errors, uncertainties or plain lies in their evidence. The prosecution may also present other evidence such as CCTV footage, tapes or transcripts of interviews, photographs or objects (such as weapons).

When the prosecution has called all its witnesses, unless they have failed to show any case at all for Dean to answer, it is Dean's solicitor's turn to call witnesses on his behalf. They go through the same process as the prosecution witnesses, giving evidence and then being cross-examined, this time by the prosecution.

Should Dean give evidence himself? He does not have to and the court cannot assume that he is guilty if he does not. Dean and his solicitor discuss this at length because there are many factors to consider. If Dean does give evidence, the CPS lawyer will ask him very challenging questions. Although the court will not allow bullying, nonetheless it can feel intimidating. If Dean does give evidence, he must stay calm and polite.

After the evidence is complete, there are legal submissions. Dean's solicitor emphasises all the evidence in Dean's favour and makes legal arguments.

The magistrates then retire to consider their verdict.

PRESS AND PUBLIC

Youth Courts are not open to the public. The only people in court are those directly involved in the case, anyone specifically authorised by the court, and the media, although they cannot report the name, address, school or other identifying details or pictures of the defendant or other young people in the case. The court can lift these reporting restrictions if appropriate to avoid injustice to the young person (e.g. to allow accurate information to be published if misleading reports are already circulating) or if it is in the public interest (which is not the same as being interesting to the public). In practice, the media rarely attend Youth Courts.

Crown Court

Only young people charged with very serious offences go to Crown Court. If this affects young people in your care, both you and they will need specialist help, advice and support, and a lot of preparation.

Crown Court cases are heard by a judge and jury. The jury decides whether the defendant is guilty and the judge presides over the case, deciding issues of law and procedure and passing sentence if the defendant is convicted.

Procedures can be adjusted to enable a young defendant to participate in the trial. For example, adult defendants sit in the dock but young people are often allowed to sit next to their barristers and their parents or carers. The court day may be shorter than usual and more breaks allowed, particularly if a young defendant is tired or unduly stressed. Plain language is used and efforts made to ensure that young defendants understand what is going on.

However, Crown Courts are by their very nature more formal and intimidating than Youth Courts. The judge sits on high and the judge and barristers usually wear wigs and gowns. Crown Courts are open to the public and there are no automatic restrictions on media reports, although the judge has the discretion to impose them.

'Special measures'[3] to help young witnesses giving evidence in Crown Courts do not apply to young defendants.

Points for practice

As a carer, you can help young defendants by:

- making sure you understand what is happening yourself – if you are not clear, they have little chance

- ensuring they have age-appropriate information

- visiting court before the hearing so you and they know where it is and what it looks like

- keeping a careful record of all court dates and appointments with lawyers, the YOT and others, and make sure the young people keep every one and get there on time

- making sure they have a lawyer and co-operate fully

- encouraging them to co-operate fully with the YOT

- informing the YOT and the young people's solicitor if they have special needs or require any facilities or services to help them participate and have a fair trial

- offering them moral and practical and emotional support without colluding

- helping them express their views

- encouraging them to dress smartly and behave respectably

- being prepared to be a taxi service and to make practical arrangements (e.g. time off school, catching up with school work)

- encouraging them to speak up and answer questions, while staying calm and respectful.[4]

---

3   For more details of special measures, see Chapter 16.

4   Young defendants whose ability to give oral evidence is compromised because of their level of intellectual ability or social functioning will be eligible to have an intermediary to help them when s104 Coroners and Justice Act 2009 is implemented. At the time of writing, it has not been decided when this will happen.

Chapter 14

Sentencing

Guilty as charged

The verdict is 'guilty'. Now the court must decide what to do with the young offender and choose, in the rather unfortunate jargon, the right 'disposal'. The objective(s) might be:

- punishment and retribution – to make offenders pay their debt to society
- deterrence – to put the offender and others off offending
- rehabilitation – to bring the offender back into society a reformed character.

In cases involving young people, the court must also try to prevent further offending and consider the offender's welfare. The court often has a range of options to try to find the right formula in each case.

Reports

Sometimes the YOT is asked for a 'same day' or oral report and the court proceeds straight to sentencing. If a full pre-sentence report is ordered, the young offender usually continues to be remanded on bail or in local authority accommodation while enquiries are made and the report written. Obviously, it would be foolish not to co-operate – that is only likely to lead to a harsher sentence. Foster carers have an important role in helping the young person to see sense.

Reports are to help the court choose the right sentence, so they include information about the offence (nature, seriousness, circumstances, impact on the victim, etc.) and offender (relevant personal circumstances, attitude to the offence, risk of re-offending, suitability of various sentencing options, etc.).

Choosing the right sentence

The term 'sentence' does not necessarily mean custody – it refers to any of the available orders (except an absolute or conditional discharge).

Sometimes the court has no choice – some sentences are mandatory. Even where the court does have discretion, there are limits:

- The Youth Court has lesser powers than the Crown Court.

- There are maximum penalties specified for different offences.

- There are age limits for different types of sentence, going by age at conviction (not the time of the offence).

Within those parameters, the court decides which option to choose by looking at the offence and the offender.

Elements of the offence
SERIOUSNESS

The court considers how serious the offence was. This depends partly on how much harm was or could have been caused: stealing a thousand pounds is more serious than stealing a fiver.

Seriousness can also depend on the offender's level of culpability. Generally speaking, intention is more serious than recklessness, which in turn is more serious than negligence.

> Rob has a grudge against Sam. He takes a weapon and sets out to really hurt him. The injuries he causes are premeditated and absolutely intentional.
>
> Trish gets into a fight with Uta. It wasn't planned but, once it starts, Trish knows that she is likely to hurt Uta and she doesn't care. She is reckless about how much harm she does.
>
> During an argument, Vic pushes Will hard. Will loses his balance and falls down a flight of stairs, suffering significant injuries. Vic is negligent – a reasonable person would have foreseen the danger.
>
> Each victim's injuries may be equally serious but the perpetrator's culpability is very different.

AGGRAVATION AND MITIGATION

Aggravating factors make an offence more serious; mitigating factors make it less serious, or at least more understandable.

> Andrew set out deliberately to steal from a shop, visiting it several times to work out where the security cameras were and planning how to distract the staff. Ben did not go out intending to steal, but, when a woman left her handbag open on a seat in the bus, he saw her purse and could not resist the temptation to take it. He acted on the spur of the moment.
>
> Both boys are thieves. But Andrew's offence is aggravated by premeditation. Ben's offence was an opportunistic crime; its spontaneity is a mitigating factor.
>
> Cassie assaults Donna, causing actual bodily harm. Cassie lost her temper after the latest incident of months of bullying over her speech impairment. The provocation is a mitigating factor.

Offences can be aggravated by:

- being premeditated or planned

- using a weapon

- targeting a vulnerable victim

- being motivated by hatred based on race, religion, sexuality or disability

- being committed while out on bail.

Offender's characteristics

Courts try to fit the punishment not only to the crime but to the criminal. Two young people may commit the same crime in the same circumstances but come out with a different sentence because of differences between them as individuals. Factors include the following:

PREVIOUS CHARACTER

Was this a first offence? Was it out of character? Or was it part of a pattern of increasingly deviant behaviour?

REMORSE

What is the young people's attitude to the offence? Are they truly remorseful? How are they showing this (a grudging 'sorry' will not do)? Do they really understand and regret the impact of their behaviour? Foster carers can help young people come to an appropriate understanding and attitude towards their behaviour, and this may directly influence the sentence they receive.

AGE

The younger the offenders are, the more allowance is likely to be made. Offenders' maturity, whatever their age, is also a consideration.

PERSONAL BACKGROUND AND CIRCUMSTANCES

What individual pressures or difficulties do the young people have? Is there a history of abuse or neglect? Are there family or other circumstances that might explain their behaviour (e.g. family break-up)? Do they now have positive influences, perhaps from foster carers? Do they have a job, place at college, constructive activities or hobbies? Are they tackling their substance abuse problems?

CO-OPERATION WITH THE POLICE AND AUTHORITIES

The court can take into account a young person's behaviour from arrest onwards. It will have a different attitude to someone who co-operates with police and the YOT, attends court on time, and is smart and respectful, than to a stroppy, difficult young person who misses appointments and refuses to participate. Foster carers can help young people to see sense.

GUILTY PLEA

Credit is always given for pleading guilty and the earlier this is done the greater the 'discount'. This is because offenders are owning up to what they have done (even if it is at the last minute before trial and when conviction is inevitable) and, by avoiding a full trial, they are saving court time and public money as well as avoiding inconvenience and distress to victims and witnesses. Sometimes, the best advice to a young person is to own up.

The victim's input

Courts can consider a 'victim impact statement' where the victim outlines the consequences of the offence for him. However, the victim cannot decide the sentence. If they wish, victims can be directly involved in sentences that include an element of restorative justice.

Sentences

Types of sentence

Broadly speaking, there are four categories of disposal:

1. Discharge (absolute or conditional).

2. Financial penalty (fine).

3. Community orders (referral order or Youth Rehabilitation Order (YRO)).

4. Custodial sentence (detention and training order).

Discharge

An absolute discharge is the lightest possible outcome on conviction. There are no further consequences; the prosecution and finding of guilt are enough of a punishment in themselves.

A conditional discharge is, as the name suggests, a discharge that is dependent on young people staying out of trouble for a specified period up to three years. If they re-offend in that time, they can be sentenced again for the first crime. In practice, few conditional discharges are handed out, because there must be 'exceptional circumstances' before a court can choose this option if the young person has received a final warning in the previous two years.

Fines

The maximum fine for a young person is usually £1000, the amount reflecting both the seriousness of the offence and the offender's means to pay. Fines for under 16s are normally paid by parents or carers (the local authority if the young person is in care – not the foster carers personally).

Community orders

These orders restrict young people's freedom to spend time as they wish, without going so far as imposing a custodial sentence. The two choices are a referral order or a YRO.

REFERRAL ORDER

Referral orders are for young offenders who plead guilty and who are at a relatively early stage in their criminal 'career'. They operate on restorative justice principles aiming to make offenders take responsibility for their actions, make reparations and reintegrate into society.

The court must impose a referral order (unless the offence is so serious that custody is essential or so minor that an absolute discharge is appropriate) where:

- the offender is aged between 10 and 17

- the offender pleaded guilty

- it is the offender's first conviction (or a second offence provided a referral order has not been imposed before)

- the offence is 'imprisonable' (that is, an adult offender could be sent to prison).

Referral orders are usually only made once: a second referral order is only possible in exceptional circumstances if the YOT recommends it.

Referral orders last between 3 and 12 months according to the seriousness of the offence.

What happens under a referral order?

The court does not determine what actually happens under a referral order; as the name suggests, the case is referred on to a Youth Offender Panel. A YOT worker is allocated to the young offender as soon as the order is made. He explains the process to the offender and the parents or carers and prepares a report.

> Fifteen-year-old Jane is in foster care because her mother could not cope with her challenging behaviour. She pleaded guilty to a number of charges including criminal damage and being drunk and disorderly. It is her first time in court, so the court must make a referral order. Within 20 days, Jane has to attend a meeting of the Youth Offender Panel. Her carer goes with her because the court

ordered a local authority representative to be present.

The meeting is not held in a police station or YOT office but in the village hall. The members of Youth Offender Panel introduce themselves. There are three volunteer representatives of the local community (there must be at least two), recruited and trained by the YOT. With them is a member of the YOT who is not part of the Panel but is there to give them advice.

Victim involvement

A YOT worker contacts the victim, sensitively, shortly after the order is made, and meets the victim to explain the options and the process. Victims may choose to attend the meeting or have their views reported. Participation is entirely voluntary and based on informed consent. Victims are entitled to support through the process.

> Jane's meeting is attended by Mrs Kamal, who runs a playgroup in the building Jane vandalised. Mrs Kamal explains how upset she was to find windows smashed and foul language spray painted over the walls. She tells Jane how she had to cancel the playgroup for two days, and how distressed the children were that their special space had been spoiled. She explains how much inconvenience was caused and how much it cost to put everything right. Mrs Kamal asks Jane why she did it. Jane explains it was just for a laugh because she was drunk. She thought because it was just a building it didn't matter. Jane's foster mother is amazed to see that, for the first time, Jane (who was confident, even cocky at court) starts to show real remorse and begins to cry. Jane apologises to Mrs Kamal.

Contract

The meeting agrees a contract with two objectives:

1. Making reparation to the victim or the wider community (an apology, financial compensation or community service such as cleaning off graffiti or helping elderly people).

2. Reducing the risk of re-offending through a programme of activities or interventions, allowing for the young person's other commitments (such as education, training or religious observance).

If the court seriously considered a custodial sentence, an intensive contract is appropriate involving intensive supervision and support.

Interventions are designed to tackle the key risk factors identified in the YOT report. They might include mentoring, sports, anger management, family counselling, substance misuse programmes, cognitive behaviour therapy, going to an attendance centre, or a curfew (although an electronic tag is not an available option).

The length of the order runs from when the contract is signed. Activities agreed under the contract should start within five days.

> Jane is surprised to find that the contract is not just imposed on her: it is a real negotiation and she is able to contribute her ideas. The contract is drawn up in plain English. It is agreed as follows:
>
> - As reparation Jane will write a letter of apology to Mrs Kamal and all the parents and children of the playgroup.
>
> - Jane will help to re-paint the playgroup's kitchen.
>
> - She will volunteer at the playgroup during the school holidays.
>
> - To prevent re-offending, she will attend a programme to address her drinking.
>
> - She will have a mentor to give her a more positive role model.
>
> - She will attend an arts project to find a constructive outlet for her feelings.

Progress meetings should be held regularly, at least every three months. The young person can request a progress meeting.

Lack of co-operation

If the young offender refuses to go to the Youth Offender Panel meeting, the matter goes back to the court, which can decide on a different sort of sentence for the offence. The court will be unimpressed by the failure to co-operate with its original order.

If a contract is agreed but the young person fails to comply, the YOT worker contacts the young person, then (assuming there is no satisfactory explanation) a Panel meeting is convened. Sometimes, the contract needs to be reconsidered. But if there is no reasonable justification for non-compliance, the case can go back to court where a different sentence can be imposed for the original crime.

End of the contract

A final meeting is held in the last month of the contract period in order to review the young person's compliance and give feedback. If the contract has been fully complied with, the order is discharged. The conviction becomes 'spent' straight away, so it does not have to be declared, for example, on job applications (although it will still show up on enhanced CRB checks).

THE YRO

> Four young people have been convicted by the Youth Court after pleading not guilty, so a referral order is not an option. Their offences are serious enough to warrant some restriction on their liberty, but not custody.
>
> Alex comes from a dysfunctional family, heavily involved in crime. The magistrates want him to live with better role models and to keep away from his criminal associates.
>
> Barnie's offences are all linked to his drug habit. Tackling that problem is the key to addressing his criminal behaviour.
>
> Cleo's offending seems to be due to her mental health difficulties. The magistrates want her to have psychiatric or psychological treatment.
>
> David is not in school and gets into trouble because he is bored. He needs to get back into education and engaged in constructive activities.
>
> A single sentence, the YRO, allows the magistrates to tailor-make an order for each of them.

This single standard community sentence has replaced a whole range of orders that previously existed.[1] It is available for any offence and can be imposed any number of times. It lasts for up to three years.

It is one single sentence, but it allows a proportionate and flexible approach with the court devising an order for each young offender from a range of 18 different 'requirements'. A pre-sentence report helps the court choose the right option(s) according to the:

- seriousness of the offence

- court's objectives

---

1   Before 30 November 2009. These were: action plan order, attendance centre order, community rehabilitation order, community punishment order, curfew order, drug treatment and testing order, exclusion order and supervision order.

- risk of re-offending

- offender's ability to comply

- availability of programmes in the local area.

The potential requirements are:

- residence (where the court believes that offending is linked to the young person's home life)

  o residence requirement (requiring the young person to live with a specified person or at a specified place)

  o local authority residence requirement (requiring the young person to live in accommodation provided by the local authority – possibly foster care – for up to six months)

- activities

  o activity requirement (participating in specified activities, possibly residential, for a set number of days; these may include an element of reparation)

  o unpaid work (for 16- and 17-year-olds only – between 40 and 240 hours work within 12 months)

  o prohibited activity requirement (prohibiting a particular activity or association with particular people)

  o programme requirement (participation in a systematic programme of activities, possibly residential, such as a victim awareness or knife crime prevention programme)

  o attendance centre (often on Saturdays, for a set number of hours – up to 12 hours for under 14s, 12–24 hours for 14–16-year-olds and 12–36 hours for over 16s)

- supervision (the young person has to meet with the nominated supervisor on an agreed basis)

- restrictions

  o curfew requirement (the young person must stay in a specified place for between 2 and 12 hours a day for a maximum of 6 months – appropriate where the criminal activity happens at a certain time of day, usually at night)

- o electronic monitoring requirement (tagging – linked with a curfew)

- o exclusion requirement (prohibiting the young person from going to a specified place for a specified period of up to three months)

- education (for under 16s to attend education, be it school, pupil referral unit, college, alternative education provision or home tutoring)

- health (provided the young person is willing to accept treatment)

  - o mental health treatment (psychiatric or psychological, possibly as an in-patient; the court must receive expert evidence before imposing this)

  - o drug treatment, possibly residential

  - o drug testing (alongside drug treatment)

  - o intoxicating substance treatment (including alcohol, solvents, etc.)

- for serious cases where a custodial sentence was a serious possibility (and, if aged under 15, the young person is a persistent offender)

  - o intensive supervision and surveillance, including an extended activity requirement for 90–180 days, supervision, curfew and tagging and any other requirements. Required contacts can be for up to 25 hours a week for the first couple of months. Activities must include education, particularly basic skills, training and employment, tackling offending behaviour, making reparations, developing interpersonal skills and family support

  - o intensive fostering – a requirement for the offender to live with foster carers for up to a year.

Intensive fostering

This is only available if the local authority has specialist provision available. Intensive fostering is based on the model 'Multi-dimensional treatment foster care', a highly structured programme where a young person earns points to gain privileges rewarding appropriate behaviour and moves up levels of increasing autonomy. Young people on this programme are the only children in the foster home.

A whole support team works with the young people to improve their social skills, behaviour and attitude. At the same time, work is done with the young people's families to improve their functioning. Foster carers are specially selected and trained in the multi-dimensional model, offending behaviour, child and adolescent development, dealing with challenging behaviour, communicating with young people, risk management, drug use, the legal system and the work of the YOT. They receive daily supervision to discuss the young people's behaviour and address problems before they become out of control.

Before specifying an intensive fostering requirement, the court must be satisfied that the young offenders' home lives played a significant role in their offending behaviour and that intensive fostering will help their rehabilitation. The court must consult the young person, their parents or guardians (if practicable) and the local authority. The young person must have been legally represented or refused representation when the court was considering this order.

All YROs with an intensive fostering requirement must also include supervision, and may include any of the other requirements as well. The intensive fostering team must provide weekly progress reports to the YOT and must meet regularly. The YOT must be involved in looked after children reviews and in the planning process for the young person.

Who manages the YRO?

An officer of the YOT or probation is appointed to manage the YRO, putting the requirements into effect, promoting the young person's compliance and, if necessary, taking steps to enforce the order.

Breaching a YRO

If you are fostering young people who are subject to YROs, do everything possible to encourage them to comply. If they find the terms of the YRO difficult or if there is a significant change in their circumstances (e.g. they start a college course and so cannot attend a specified activity), they must talk to their YOT worker rather than just not turn up. You may need to take the initiative on their behalf.

The first failure to comply without a good reason leads to a warning. The case could go back to court on a second breach, but usually two warnings are allowed. On the third breach, the case goes back to the court, which can:

- allow the YRO to continue with no further sanction

- allow the YRO to continue and impose a fine for the breach

- amend the terms of the YRO

- revoke the YRO and re-sentence the offender, looking at all available options. This could mean custody if the original offence was serious or if the breach is 'wilful and persistent' even if the original crime was not an imprisonable offence.

YROs are 'spent' one year after conviction or at the end of the order, whichever is later.

Custodial sentences

Courts must consider a full pre-sentence report before passing a custodial sentence. Custody is a last resort, to be used only when no other sentence is appropriate (not even a YRO with intensive supervision and support, or intensive fostering), generally because the offence has caused really serious harm. Courts are conscious of the high risk to young people in detention and must explain why only a custodial sentence will do.

There are three types of custodial sentences:

1. Detention and training orders (12–17-year-olds).

2. Long-term custody for very serious crimes (10–17-year-olds) – this sentence, passed by a Crown Court, can be up to the same maximum length as for an adult.

3. Detention 'at Her Majesty's pleasure' for homicide (10–17-year-olds) – this sentence, passed by a Crown Court, is the youth equivalent to a life sentence for adults.

Few young people commit crimes of such gravity as to warrant long-term custody or detention at Her Majesty's pleasure. If one of your young people receives a custodial sentence, it is most likely to be a detention and training order.

DETENTION AND TRAINING ORDER

This order is available for 12–17-year-olds convicted of an offence for which an adult could be imprisoned. The Youth Court can only impose this on 12–14-year-olds if they are persistent offenders. The order must be made for the shortest time appropriate to the seriousness of the offence. It can be for 4, 6, 8, 10, 12, 18 or 24 months. Half is served in custody and the other half in the community under supervision of a probation officer, social worker or YOT officer. The release from custody can be brought forward or put back depending on the young person's progress against an agreed sentence plan while in custody.

The custodial part of the sentence may be spent in the following facilities.

- A secure children's home, for boys aged 12–14 (or up to 16 if they are vulnerable) and girls up to 16. These are usually small units run by social services departments on a welfare basis with a high staff ratio. They also house young people who are there for their own welfare without having committed offences.

- A secure training centre (STC), for offenders up to 17. These centres are suitable for vulnerable young people because they have a high staff ratio and provide a constructive, education-focused regime.

- A YOI, for over 15-year-olds. These are run by the prison service or private providers. They are larger units with lower staffing ratios than STCs and less able to provide individualised care.

Maintaining links with the outside world is vital for young people in custody. Visits from foster carers or former carers can be a lifeline and should form a key part of the plan for a detained young person.

As soon as the sentence is passed, and especially towards the end of the time in custody, preparations must be made to settle the young people back into the community and avoid further offending on their return. If they are returning to foster care after their time in detention, foster carers have a crucial role to play in planning.

Points for practice

- Understand the outline of how the sentencing process works – then you can explain it to a young person.

- Always encourage a young person to co-operate with reports and assessments – failure to co-operate is likely to result in a heavier sentence.

- Liaise closely with the YOT and all professionals involved in the case – team working is crucial.

- Support a young person on a community sentence – practically and emotionally – to make sure they comply with requirements.

- Seek help and support for yourself.

Chapter 15

Anti-Social Behaviour

'Anti-social behaviour' includes behaviour that is not criminal but just a nuisance to society, like playing loud music, rowdy drunkenness and general loutishness.

Acceptable Behaviour Contracts (ABCs)

If young people are behaving anti-socially but still at a relatively low level, voluntary written ABCs can be negotiated with them and their parents or carers to divert them from further trouble. ABCs are creations of practical experience, not statute. Because they are not strictly connected with the criminal justice system, ABCs can apply to children of any age, including those under ten. Various agencies can be involved, depending on the circumstances, including the YOT, housing, education and children's social care.

Under ABCs, young people acknowledge the negative effect of their behaviour on others, agree to stop unacceptable behaviour and undertake positive activities, like attending school, a youth project, or a drug or alcohol programme. ABCs can also incorporate an element of restorative justice.

> Nine-year-old Desmond is misbehaving at school and neighbours have repeatedly complained about him to the local community warden. He and his mother attend an ABC meeting, where the effect of his behaviour on others is spelled out. He is told how his behaviour has to change or he will get into more trouble. Desmond agrees that his behaviour has been unacceptable. He signs a contract written in simple, clear terms promising not to shout rude words at people, not to climb on the school roof again, not to spit in the street and not to break windows. He promises to write to the head teacher to say sorry for climbing on the roof. He also promises to go to school regularly.

> For the six months of Desmond's contract, agencies keep an eye on his behaviour. At the end of that time, because Desmond has kept to his agreement, he receives a letter of congratulation.

Viewed positively, an ABC is an early intervention to prevent more serious problems; the downside is that failure to observe an ABC can be cited in an application for a stronger measure like an ASBO.

Anti-Social Behaviour Orders (ASBOs)

ASBOs are only available for over ten-year-olds. They are usually applied for in stand-alone proceedings, but they can also be made by a criminal court on conviction.

Anti-social behaviour is behaviour that causes or is likely to cause harassment, alarm or distress to another person or people (not members of the same household). The definition is deliberately wide and flexible.

Local authorities, housing authorities and the police all have power to apply for ASBOs. One agency should take the lead, in consultation with the others to avoid conflict or duplication. If an ASBO is sought against a young person, the YOT must be involved from the outset and should carry out an assessment of the young person's circumstances and needs. A parent or carer must attend court with a defendant who is under 16.

To get an order the applicant agency must prove that:

- the defendant acted in an anti-social manner (whether once or repeatedly)

- the behaviour caused harassment, alarm or distress, or was likely to do so (even if there is no evidence that it in fact did and whether or not the defendant meant to upset anybody)

- an order is necessary to protect people from further anti-social behaviour.

ASBOs are civil orders, not criminal ones so the very strict rules of evidence for criminal proceedings do not apply. The court can take second-hand 'hearsay' evidence into account.

> Residents of an estate have been terrorised by a gang of youths who have been vandalising the buildings and cars parked outside, urinating in lifts, blocking the way when people try to get past, shouting abuse and generally making residents' lives a misery.

People are scared to leave their flats at night. The housing authority decides to act in a co-ordinated effort with other agencies including the police. It organises a public meeting, the housing officer visits residents to take statements and video cameras are installed to record incidents.

Many residents are too afraid to go to court to give evidence although they want something done. Because hearsay evidence is allowed, the housing officer can present their information to court without giving their names or addresses. This hearsay evidence is backed up by the officer's own observations, by other witnesses such as the community police officer and by the video footage. Some residents are prepared to give evidence in person. The authority gives them support and they may benefit from 'special measures'[1] such as giving evidence from behind a screen instead of having to face the defendants.

Standard of proof

In normal civil proceedings, the applicant has to prove the case 'on the balance of probabilities' (that is, more likely than not). But ASBOs are peculiar because, although they are civil proceedings, the criminal standard of proof applies, thanks to an important test case in the House of Lords.[2] The authority applying for the order must prove its case 'beyond reasonable doubt'.

ASBOs involving young defendants are heard in the Magistrates' Court (the Youth Court only deals with crime), although the magistrates hearing the case are often members of the Youth Bench who are used to dealing with young people. Unlike criminal cases, civil cases do not attract reporting restrictions – on the contrary, publicity is often positively sought for ASBOs. Their objective is to stop a nuisance, so publishing names and descriptions can assist in monitoring and enforcing orders. So whereas a young criminal's details may not be published, a young person who has behaved in an anti-social but sub-criminal way can have his full details in all the local papers.

---

1   For more information on special measures for vulnerable and intimidated witnesses, see Chapter 16.

2   McCann (*R v Crown Court at Manchester ex parte McCann [FC] and Others [FC]*). Available at www.publications.parliament.uk/pa/ld200102/ldjudgmt/jd021017/cling-1.htm, accessed on 6 July 2010.

What is in an ASBO?

It is up to the court to decide what goes into an ASBO depending on the circumstances of each case. It must explain the order clearly to the defendant and give him a copy.

The order prohibits specified acts, covering all the anti-social behaviour complained of, in a defined area. The order should be:

- reasonable and proportionate

- realistic and practical

- clear, concise and easy to understand

- specific about times and places.

ASBOs are prohibitions – they specify what people must not do, not what they must do.

How long does an ASBO last?

The law sets a minimum term of two years. There is no maximum; an ASBO can be indefinite. ASBOs for young people must be reviewed every year.

Implications of ASBOs

An ASBO is not a criminal record because it is a civil order, not a criminal one.

However, breach of an ASBO is a criminal offence even if the original behaviour for which the ASBO was made was not criminal. Breaches by young people are tried in the Youth Court. On conviction, the full range of possible sentences (except conditional discharge) is available right up to a detention and training order for offenders aged over 12 (provided they are persistent offenders if they are under 14), although custody should be used only as a last resort in serious cases.

Individual Support Orders (ISOs)

These can be coupled with ASBOs for young people if the court feels that it would help prevent further anti-social behaviour. Whereas the ASBO itself only contains prohibitions, the ISO imposes positive requirements designed to tackle the underlying causes of the anti-social behaviour. ISOs are civil orders, which can last for up to six months.

Points for practice

- Addressing anti-social behaviour can stop a young person descending to a life of crime. Carers have a crucial role to play.

- Good working relationships with your local YOT are invaluable.

- Do everything you can to encourage a young person on an ASBO to comply with the order and avoid more serious consequences.

Chapter 16

Young Victims and Witnesses – Evidence and Compensation

Child victims of crime

Children's evidence

There is no minimum age to give evidence. Everyone is competent to be a witness, whatever their age, unless, even with the 'special measures' available to help them,[1] they are unable to understand questions asked or to give intelligible answers.

It is true that the younger or more vulnerable (through disabilities, mental ill-health or emotional trauma) victims are, the harder it is for the system to protect them. But it can be done: in 2009, Steven Barker was convicted of rape when a four-year-old girl gave evidence about abuse dating back to when she was only two, becoming the youngest witness ever to appear at the Old Bailey.[2]

Disclosures

Sometimes the first time children feel safe enough to disclose what has happened is when they are settled in a foster home and confide in the carer they trust. This can come out of the blue – a child in foster care voluntarily because of a parent's ill-health may unexpectedly disclose sexual abuse. Spontaneous disclosures are highly significant and can be

---

1   For more details on special measures, see p.201–2.
2   *R v Barker* [2010] EWCA Crim 4, Court of Appeal.

191

powerful evidence, but they must be handled properly. Your training and preparation as a foster carer should cover what to do – and what not to do – in such situations.

If children make a disclosure we want to allow them to talk – the last thing we want to do is silence them because they may never venture into such delicate territory again. Letting them talk is one thing; questioning them is quite another. Investigation is not part of the fostering task. Interviewing children is a specialist job to be carried out only by police officers and social workers with specific training, and following detailed guidelines.[3] If an untrained person asks questions the evidence may be contaminated and might even be thrown out of court, leaving children unprotected and feeling they have not been believed, and leaving a perpetrator unpunished.

Don't

- stop children talking ('Hold on a minute while I get a pen, I want to write this all down')

- judge or show revulsion ('How awful! What an appalling man your father is!')

- promise not to tell – in fact children must understand this information has to be passed on to keep them safe

- launch into an interrogation – avoid leading questions at all costs ('It was Daddy who hurt you, wasn't it?').

Do

- stay calm
- listen and soak up what children have to say
- empathise and reassure them
- explain to them that you must pass the information on
- contact children's social workers and your fostering officer urgently
- carefully record everything while it is fresh in your mind.

---

3   For more detail, see p.194.

Record exactly what happened and what was said. Context is important: what was the child doing when the disclosure was made? Was it prompted by anything (such as something said on TV) or was it completely out of the blue?

Quote the child's own words as closely as you can remember them. A diary recording that a five-year-old 'disclosed that he had been repeatedly anally abused' is not helpful – it does not tell us what the child said, but the carer's interpretation, which may or may not be sound.

Record your own responses and any questions you asked. This will help to show whether the disclosure was spontaneous or whether it was prompted or coached.

> Eight-year-old Ben tells his foster mother Carol that Dan (his step-father) did rude things to him. Carol remains calm, resists the temptation to question Ben but lets him say what he wants to say. What follows is a clear disclosure of sexual abuse. Carol reassures Ben – his welfare is her first priority – but at the first opportunity she writes down word-for-word everything he said, contacts Ben's social worker and her own link worker.
>
> As sexual abuse is both a child protection and a criminal matter, the social worker contacts the police child protection unit. They arrange a joint visit to Ben at the foster home. Carol lets Ben know that his social worker is coming round with a colleague to see him, but she is careful not to worry him or to prepare him so much that she could in any way be accused of coaching him.
>
> The police officer (in plain clothes) and social worker do not conduct a full interview at the foster home – doing so might jeopardise the evidence – but they listen to Ben and do not stop him if he wants to talk. Their objective is to get preliminary information about the disclosure and about Ben so that they can decide on further investigations. They talk in detail to Carol and look at her notes of the disclosure – they want to know what Ben said, when, what prompted it, his demeanour and his reactions afterwards.
>
> They also listen carefully to Carol's views about how to approach a formal interview with Ben. They want to know about:
>
> - any special needs, learning difficulties or physical disabilities Ben may have
>
> - his memory and attention span
>
> - any special interests to help build rapport and engage him

- how good he is at understanding questions and expressing himself, and how best to communicate with him

- any special words he uses, especially for parts of the body

- his emotional state and behaviour

- names (including nicknames) of his family members and others

- any other information Carol can give to help plan for the interview.

Carol asks what to do if, in the meantime, Ben wants to talk about the abuse or if he makes any more disclosures. She is advised not to stop him talking if he is freely recalling what happened, but not to prompt any discussions or to question him. She must record in detail anything he says and inform the social worker as soon as possible.

Detailed official guidance for police and social workers seeking evidence from children and other vulnerable witnesses is given in *Achieving Best Evidence in Criminal Proceedings: Guidance on Interviewing Victims and Witnesses and Using Special Measures*.[4] Sometimes, interviews with children are simply referred to as 'ABE' interviews, reflecting the guidance title.

Planning an investigation includes considering the child's:

- age

- any special needs or characteristics

- language and culture

- gender

- (for older young people) sexuality.

These factors may affect the choice of interviewer and the way the interview is carried out. It may also aid in understanding the child's answers and behaviour – for example, making direct eye contact may be a sign of honesty and openness in one culture but be rude and aggressive in another.

In planning an investigation, police and social workers should seek information and views from others involved with the child, including

---

4   CPS (2007). Available at www.cps.gov.uk/Publications/docs/Achieving_Best_Evidence_FINAL.pdf, accessed on 6 July 2010.

parents (unless this is inappropriate in the circumstances). For children in foster care, carers have a very important contribution to make.

Video-recorded interviews

An interview recorded on video is the usual method of seeking and recording information from children who are victims of or witnesses to crime. Videos can be very powerful evidence, showing a child's body language, demeanour and reactions in a way that a written statement never could. However, videos are not always appropriate – a child whose abuse has been filmed may be traumatised by a video camera. As carer, you may have picked this up from the child's words or reactions – pass this on, even if it is just a hunch. The last thing anyone wants is for the investigation to compound the abuse.

Other young people find it very difficult to talk about their abuse, and may find it easier to write things down or express themselves in another way. Pass on your thoughts and observations to the police and social workers.

The interview is:

- part of the investigation of an alleged crime, and

- the child's evidence in chief if the case goes to a criminal trial.

It may also be used in care proceedings. However, it most definitely is not a therapeutic interview. Its purpose is to obtain information from the child, not to counsel or console.

PREPARING FOR AN INTERVIEW

The child needs to know in outline what is going to happen without rehearsing the interview. Both the child and carer should be told:

- when and where it will take place

- how long it is likely to last

- who will be there

- what it is for

- why it will be recorded

- who might see the recording
- what will be discussed, without going into detail.

NO REWARDS OR INDUCEMENTS

Children must not be offered any rewards or inducements for co-operating with interviews or answering any questions. Be very careful – something you might not mean to be a reward might feel like one to the child – 'if you're good at the interview tomorrow, we'll go for a pizza afterwards' might mean 'say the right thing and you'll have a pizza'.

We can unconsciously signal to children when they give the 'right' answer by smiling or nodding, or through our tone of voice. Children also easily pick up that they have given the 'wrong' answer if they do not get approval or if the question is asked again in another way. Coaching is not always overt or intentional – children pick up very subtle clues as to what we 'want' them to say.

Sometimes children do not disclose because they have nothing to say: a denial must be treated with the same respect as a disclosure. Sometimes children disclose, then think better of it and decide never to repeat it. Sometimes they disclose then retract. We must not let our adult frustration at a jeopardised prosecution get in the way of the child's right to disclose or not and to be cared for no matter what.

INTERVIEW SUITES

Usually video-recorded interviews take place in specially designed rooms that are as comfortable and homely as possible. Toys are available but usually kept out of sight at first so as not to distract the child. Video cameras are usually fixed on a wall and operated from an adjacent room.

WHO CONDUCTS THE INTERVIEW?

Interviewing children is a skilled task requiring specific training. Usually either the police officer or the social worker takes the lead, with the other person monitoring in an adjacent room and communicating with the interviewer via an earpiece, suggesting questions, pointing out apparent confusions or miscommunications, prompting to cover contradictions or gaps, or highlighting a child's demeanour.

DOES THE CARER SIT IN?
It is generally best to have only the interviewer and the child in the room in order to avoid any confusion or suggestion of 'contamination'. Some children do not want their carers in the building at all, others are happy to know that they are in the next room waiting for them as soon as it is all over. Occasionally a child cannot cope with an interview without a carer present. In such cases, the carer may be asked to come in; however, the carer must not take an active part in the interview and must remain neutral, not giving even the most subtle sign to encourage the child to disclose.

WHAT IF THE CHILD DOES NOT SPEAK ENGLISH?
Part of the planning of the interview includes arranging, where appropriate, for an accredited interpreter of a spoken or signed language, or other communication system. Trained intermediaries are available, if needed, to help facilitate communication with children who are disabled.

Phases of interview

All interviews are different but they should follow the same basic pattern: introductions, rapport, free narrative, questions and close.

> The police officer, Elliot, conducts Ben's interview. The social worker Fern is in an adjoining room. Carol waits outside.
>
> Elliot starts by introducing himself and, for the benefit of the recording, states the location, date and time. He shows Ben the cameras and tells him that Fern is in the other room. Elliot and Fern check that the cameras and the earpiece are working.
>
> Elliot then starts talking to Ben about neutral topics to put him at ease and build up a rapport. They talk about football – both are Chelsea fans. Elliot encourages Ben to talk freely and not just give 'yes' or 'no' answers.
>
> Elliot also explains some ground rules, using language Ben can understand:
>
> - Elliot wasn't there when anything happened, so he needs Ben to tell him everything.
>
> - If Ben doesn't know the answer to a question, he must say so and not try to guess or make things up.

- If Ben doesn't understand anything, he must say so.

- Ben can tell Elliot anything in this room, even rude things, and he can use naughty words.

- If Elliot gets anything wrong, Ben must tell him.

Elliot then gives an example of a boy who breaks a window but tells his mother that his brother did it. He asks some questions to show that Ben knows the difference between truth and lies. Elliot stresses the importance of telling the truth.

Elliot moves on to the most important part of the interview, the 'free narrative' when he encourages Ben to talk about what happened to him. The less Elliot has to question or prompt him, the better in evidential terms.

When Ben has had a chance to express himself, Elliot asks some questions to clarify what Ben has said and to seek more details, aided by Fern's observations. Elliot keeps questions short, clear and simple, and chooses open questions whenever possible.

To round the interview off, Elliot checks that he has properly understood what Ben has said, asks him if he has any questions, thanks him for coming, then chats a little about what Ben is going to do at the weekend before ending the interview, stating the time for the benefit of the tape.

WHAT IF A CHILD DISCLOSES NOTHING?

If a child says nothing of significance during the free recall phase, the interviewer may decide to end the interview or to move on to the question phase. Open questions (e.g. 'What happened?') are best because they do not influence the answer, but closed questions giving a choice between a limited number of options (e.g. 'Was it Daddy Paul or Daddy Peter who did that?') can be appropriate, and sometimes leading questions (e.g. 'Did he touch your privates?') have to be used. For evidence, the more open the questioning, the better.

Even if children say nothing, the interviewer must still thank them for coming and not betray any frustration or displeasure.

Further interviews

Sometimes there is more than one interview, perhaps because the child's very young age or disability means that several short interviews are more appropriate than one long one, or perhaps because there are so many incidents and details to recall that it cannot all be done in one session. Sometimes the interview itself prompts further disclosures requiring a further interview.

Do cases always go to court after a video interview?

Sometimes interviews are inconclusive or contradictory, or the child appears too vulnerable or confused to justify a prosecution. Even where a video is compelling, the case may not go to court because there are many other factors to consider. As carer, you need to be kept informed of the progress of the investigation and prosecution decisions.

If children have a video interview but no prosecution results, they may feel they have not been believed, that it is their fault that the case is not going to court, or angry that the abuser is not being punished. Careful work is needed and, as carer, you must be prepared for the fall-out.

The video interview in court

The video takes the place of evidence in chief, so children do not have to go over everything again in court. But defendants still have the right to a fair trial, including testing the evidence against them, so children have to attend court for cross-examination (with the special measures described on pp.202–203 to soften the process). Videos may not spare children the whole court experience but they do:

- allow children's evidence to be recorded while events are fresh in their minds

- avoid allegations that their evidence has been tainted by the court process and

- reduce the amount of time they have to spend in court.

Videos might also be used in care proceedings or for a compensation claim.

Medical examinations

If a child's disclosure is of a physical or sexual assault, a forensic medical examination will probably follow. This is carried out as sensitively as possible, usually in a special examination suite with specially trained doctors. The child can choose the gender of the doctors, but if the child does not specify a preference, the doctors are usually female. They will carry out an examination and may have to take samples for testing (e.g. for sexually transmitted diseases) and photographs for evidence.

However skilled and sensitive the practitioners, an intimate medical examination is bound to be a difficult experience that may reawaken memories of the original abuse. The child needs considerable support from you as carer, and you need support in your own right.

Between investigations and court

There is inevitably a wait – often several months – between an interview or medical and the court case. During this time, the child and carers should be kept informed of what is going on. If you are in this situation, make sure you know whom to contact if the child makes further disclosures or retractions, or shows any significant reactions. You may need extra support to help the child cope with anxiety, stress, flashbacks or other feelings provoked by the prospect of going to court.

Therapy before trial

If a child has therapy or counselling before giving evidence in a criminal trial, the defence might argue that the evidence has become unreliable by being rehearsed, embellished and reinforced in therapy. The child's evidence could be thrown out, jeopardising the trial.

For this reason, the police and CPS should always be involved in discussions about whether a child witness should have therapy. However, it is not their decision and the effect on the trial is not the only or the main issue – the key question is the child's overall welfare, including the child's interests in the perpetrator being brought to justice.

Some types of therapy are more problematic than others – in group therapy, for example, the child might hear another child's experiences, and the defence will argue that they might have swapped stories or added details.

With careful planning, it may be possible to find a way to help the child without jeopardising the evidence.[5] Sometimes, however, it is better to abandon the prosecution rather than leave the child without therapy.

If therapy or counselling goes ahead, therapist, child and carer must all understand that it cannot be confidential. The therapist must not lead or coach the child, and may have to give evidence about the therapy at court. Any new allegations, retractions or variations in the disclosure must be reported.

Preparing for court

There is a big difference between preparing for court (which is allowed) and rehearsing evidence (which is not). It is unacceptable that some young witnesses still receive no preparation or support before going to court. There are (non-statutory) National Standards for Young Witness Preparation that should be followed.[6] A witness support service should prepare the child, including a visit to the court building. The NSPCC has produced a 'Young witness pack' and a video 'Giving evidence – what's it like?', which child and carer may view with the witness support officer.

Preparing young witnesses includes ensuring they understand:

- the court process

- the roles of the participants in the case

- their own role

- the importance of telling the truth

- possible outcomes, including adjournments, a late guilty plea, abandoned trials or an acquittal.

Before court, children have the chance to view their video interview or re-read their statement to refresh their memory.

As carer, be prepared to insist on a child receiving proper preparation and support.

---

5   There is practice guidance produced jointly by the Home Office, CPS and Department of Health (2001) *Provision of Therapy for Child Witnesses Prior to a Criminal Trial: Practice Guidance.* Available at www.cps.gov.uk/publications/prosecution/therapychild.html, accessed on 6 July 2010.

6   This is reproduced as Appendix F in the *Achieving Best Evidence* guidelines.

At court

Children should be greeted by a witness supporter at court and should have somewhere to wait separate from the defendants and their friends and family. As the children's carer, you can keep them company while they are waiting but you must not discuss the case or practise their evidence.

SPECIAL MEASURES

Witnesses aged under 17[7] are entitled to 'special measures' to help them give their evidence. A child should be involved in the choice of which measures to request, and the question should be decided well before the hearing.

The first part of children's evidence, the equivalent of evidence in chief, is given by showing the video interview. The children then have to answer cross-examination. Children under 14 answer questions without first taking the oath or affirmation; over that age they are sworn in like an adult witness. Cross-examination is always challenging. The defence lawyer has to try to show 'reasonable doubt', so will play on any apparent inconsistencies, gaps or contradictions in children's accounts or try to show that their memory is unreliable or that they are not a reliable witness in general, perhaps alleging that they had some sort of grudge against the defendant or that they have made similar allegations against other people.

As part of preparation for trial, children need to understand that the defence lawyer might seem to be calling them a liar and trying to trip them up.

Children almost always give their evidence by live TV link. The child goes into a separate room in the court building, normally accompanied by a witness supporter who is there to give support, make sure that equipment is working properly, and ensure that no-one else tries to enter the room or influence the evidence in any way. A carer is very unlikely to be allowed into the TV link room with the child[8] – the carer is likely

---

7   This will change to include all witnesses under 18 when s98 Coroners and Justice Act 2009 comes into force. At the time of writing there is no timescale for implementation.

8   When s102 Coroners and Justice Act 2009 comes into force, the court will be able to order that a specified person can accompany the child into the TV link room, and will have to take the child's wishes into account in choosing that person. At the time of writing, there is no timescale for implementation.

to be too emotionally involved and knows too much about the case, so might influence the child's answers, even subconsciously.

The child sees a TV screen showing a general view of the courtroom and a close-up of the person talking at the time – the barrister or judge talking or asking questions. In the courtroom itself, participants (including the defendant) see a TV screen showing the TV link room (confirming that only the child and supporter are present) and a close-up of the child replying to the questions. The child is only ever questioned by a lawyer or a judge – the defendant is not allowed to question or talk to the child in court.

For some children for whom a TV link is not appropriate (perhaps because the abuse was filmed), an alternative is for the child to give evidence in the courtroom itself but protected by screens so the defendant is out of view.

When adults are on trial, the court is usually open to the media and the public. When a child gives evidence, the court can exclude the public and press, leaving only those directly involved in the case and one nominated media representative.

In the Crown Court judges and barristers usually wear wigs and gowns. When a child gives evidence, these can be removed to make the process less intimidating. However, this is not always appropriate: if you ask a child what a judge looks like, the child will probably say that a judge wears a wig. Some children are more comfortable if the judge looks like a judge.

For children (and adults) with communication difficulties, evidence can be given using communication aids, such as alphabet boards, or through a trained and registered intermediary who assists communication.

After court

Sometimes there is a whirlwind of preparation and attention before court and, when it is over, everyone disappears leaving witnesses to cope on their own. Giving evidence is stressful for anyone, let alone a child. Reactions vary from one child to another, and can be complex and unpredictable – relief, euphoria, anti-climax, distress. The court experience can reawaken memories of abuse, or be a source of satisfaction and pride at speaking out, or both.

Pre-court planning should include arranging support for the child after court. Key people in the child's life, such as teachers, may need to know about the court date and be ready for a reaction. Carers bear the brunt, so make sure that you have support to call upon for yourself as well as for the child.

There is another wait between giving evidence and the verdict that can feel like being in limbo. Then there is the verdict itself. Well before the trial it should be decided who is to tell the child the outcome, when, where and how. This is not usually a job for the carer – a police officer or social worker is generally better placed – but it may be appropriate for the carer to be present. And of course the carer needs to know and understand the implications of the verdict and be ready for the reaction.

If the verdict is guilty, there may be another wait until the sentence itself is passed, if the matter is adjourned for pre-sentence reports.

Once a trial is over, there is no constraint on the type of therapy a child can be offered, so, if therapy has been on hold pending trial, it should be lined up ready to start as soon as it is over.

Compensation for victims of crime

Any innocent victim of crime of any age can claim compensation from the Criminal Injuries Compensation Authority (CICA) for any physical or mental injury (such as depression or other psychiatric illness). The scheme does not cover minor injuries because the minimum award is £1000.

Victims of crime who are not 'blameless' – for example, if they have an unspent criminal record or provoked the offence – may have their compensation reduced or receive none at all.

Compensation claims do not depend on there being a conviction or even a charge. Injuries caused in cases where there can be no prosecution – because the perpetrator is unknown or aged under ten – can still qualify for compensation. The scheme operates on the 'balance of probabilities' standard, so compensation can be awarded in some cases where there was insufficient proof for a conviction.

Normally claims have to be made within two years of the incident but exceptions can be made – for example, for someone who was a child at the time of the injury.

Claims on behalf of children have to be made by someone with PR – if they are in care, the local authority does this, sending a copy of the care order with the application.

Application

Application to the CICA is made by completing a form on paper or online. A case number is allocated and CICA staff start collecting evidence including getting in touch with the police and seeking medical reports.

Amount of compensation

Compensation for injuries is usually decided on a 'tariff' basis, a pre-determined level of award depending on seriousness. A claims officer makes the first decision and sends a notice to the applicant (or person acting on the applicant's behalf) who can choose to accept it or ask for it to be reviewed by another officer. A review may not lead to a better offer – it could result in a reduction or even no offer at all. If the applicant is still not satisfied after the review decision, appeal can be made to the independent Criminal Injuries Compensation Tribunal.

What happens to the money?

Payments to children remain in trust until they turn 18. If the young person needs money before turning 18, an advance payment may be possible for a particular purpose as long as this is solely for the young person's benefit, education or welfare – for example, funding private therapy. If a young person moves into independence under the age of 18, it is sometimes possible to receive the full amount at that time.

Once young people reach 18, they are usually entitled to the full amount, unless they have a disability or mental illness making them incapable of managing their affairs for themselves. Sometimes young people who are still relatively immature and vulnerable find themselves coming into large sums of money on their 18th birthday. Unfortunately, they may also find a sudden influx of 'friends' willing to help them spend it. Preparing young people to cope with their money and planning the management of the compensation to best effect should be an important part of pathway planning. Make sure that this is raised as an important issue at reviews.

Points for practice

- Make sure you know what to do – and what not to do – if a child discloses abuse to you.

- Contribute to planning for a video interview.

- Make sure both you and your fostered child have proper support if the child has to give evidence.

- Know who is going to tell the child the outcome of the trial.

- If no-one else raises the subject of compensation for abuse, make sure you do.

- Raise financial planning as a key issue in pathway plans for young people with a trust fund.

Part IV
Long-Term Plans

Chapter 17

Long-Term Placements

Staying together

All children and young people need a settled home. If this cannot be with their parents or extended birth family, adoption is often the preferred option. But for some, especially older children who remain attached to their birth family, adoption is not appropriate. A long-term foster placement may be the best option. Some long-term placements are planned from the start, others evolve naturally.

In law there is no difference between a foster placement that lasts for three weeks and one that lasts for ten years – fostering is fostering.

Fostering as a long-term status
PR
Foster carers never have PR in their own right, even if a child lives with them for years and feels like a full member of the family. If the placement is or becomes long term, carers should normally be delegated more decision-making powers to normalise family life, but that never changes the fact that they are carers, not parents. Birth parents and the local authority are always there.

CONTACT
Contact should be adjusted over time – what suits a 5-year-old may not still be appropriate when the child is 15. Make sure that contact is actively reviewed so it continues to meet the child's wishes and needs.

In many long-term placements, contact settles down to a comfortable pattern with parents and carers reaching a workable, even cordial, relationship. However, there is always the possibility that contact

209

will cause problems. Fostering brings with it a review mechanism for difficulties to be discussed: the social worker can act as a 'buffer' between carers and birth family and, if necessary, the matter can be taken to court for resolution.

PERMANENCE?

Legally, fostering is never permanent or secure because those who have PR (the parents of an accommodated child, or the local authority if the child is in care) always have the power to end the placement. Of course this should not happen without a proper review and the IRO should ensure that no rushed or inappropriate decisions are made. The longer the child has been in placement, the stronger the child's right to family life with the foster family, and vice versa (protected under the Human Rights Act 1998). If necessary, an application could be made to court to stop an unplanned or inappropriate move.

Equally, however much they have made a professional and moral commitment to provide a long-term placement, foster carers are not legally bound to keep a child. If there is a change of circumstances or if, despite support and effort, things simply do not work out, foster carers have the right to call an end to a placement.

SOCIAL WORKERS AND REVIEWS

Social workers and review meetings can be the bane of fostered children's lives. They can seem irrelevant and irritating if life is going well. However, there is no choice – these are legal requirements, so it is up to all concerned to make sure they are constructive. Reviews must not become 'tick box' exercises just to get them over with – after all, which of us would not benefit from periodically taking stock of our lives and planning for the future? It takes imagination and engagement to turn what seems like a nuisance into a positive and constructive feature of a young person's life.

Fostered young people can feel stigmatised and frustrated by administrative barriers to activities their friends can take part in with no problems. Sensible agreements should cover delegated consents for trips and activities, and workers may need reminding that police checks are not needed for sleep-overs.

AFTER CARE

Young people who are fostered long term often qualify for after-care services (see Chapter 18), intended and designed to help their transition into adulthood.

Legal routes to permanence

> Borsetshire's Director of Children's Services orders a review of all care orders. He is, of course, not remotely motivated by targets or funding issues and considers only the children's welfare. The review finds that some children are in settled long-term foster placements. Should they become legally part of their current foster family, discharging the care orders?
>
> Darren Smith, aged 13, was removed from his mother Enid when he was 8. His 12-year-old sister Flo has profound disabilities and lives with specialist foster carers. Darren sees her once a month.
>
> Darren has lived with his foster carers Geoff and Hazel Jones and their 10-year-old son Ivan since he came into care. Efforts to rehabilitate him to Enid's care failed and he has settled with Geoff and Hazel, seeing himself staying there forever. The couple are happy to keep him permanently, and Enid reluctantly accepts the position. Darren sees Enid once a fortnight and the relationship is important to Darren, although sometimes difficult.
>
> Darren's social worker explores whether Darren should stay with Geoff and Hazel permanently under a different sort of order: adoption, special guardianship or residence. Geoff and Hazel need to know more about what is involved, so Borsetshire funds legal advice from a Children Panel solicitor.

Adoption

An adoption order is the most drastic order a court can make: it terminates the birth parents' PR and all legal relationship with their child forever, giving exclusive PR to the adopters.

It is often the first choice for young children who cannot go home, because it provides the nearest equivalent to a full family life. In law, adopted children are treated as if they were born to their adopters. Adoption is:

- Lifelong – unlike other orders which end at 18, the effects of adoption are permanent.

- Secure – unlike other orders, adoption orders cannot be discharged or varied.

- Exclusive – unlike other orders where PR is often shared, in adoption the birth family is cut out of the picture and only the adopters have PR for the child. The adopters can change the child's name and, unless the court makes a contact order, have absolute power to decide contact.

- Comprehensive – unlike other orders, which affect only the people acquiring the order, adoption affects the whole family, ending relationships with the extended birth family and creating new relationships with the extended adoptive family.

Because it is so far-reaching, adoption has all sorts of legal safeguards. For example:

- Adoptions can only be arranged by approved adoption agencies.

- Adopters must be assessed and approved.

- There is an Adoption Panel and decision mechanism (similar to that for fostering).

- Local authorities only have the power to place a child for adoption through parental consent or a placement order made by a court.

- There must be a successful trial placement before an adoption order is made.

- The birth parent(s) must either consent to the adoption order or have their consent dispensed with by the court – for example, on the ground that the child's welfare demands adoption.

- The child's welfare throughout life is the court's paramount consideration.

Finding the right legal framework

Geoff and Hazel look at whether adoption is the right option for Darren and their own family. On the plus side, Darren would have permanence and legal security and would become a full part of the Jones family. He would come out of care and would not have a social worker or reviews any more. He would have the automatic right to take the surname Jones if he wanted.

But adoption would change all Darren's legal relationships – Enid would no longer be his mother or have any legal relationship with him. Flo would no longer be his sister, but Ivan would become his brother. Geoff and Hazel would become his legal parents. For Darren, who is well aware of his identity and has continuing relationships with Enid and Flo, this would be too much. Darren likes and wants to stay with Geoff and Hazel, but not by cutting off his birth family, even if he could carry on seeing them (which, legally, would be up to Geoff and Hazel to decide).

Geoff and Hazel also have to think about their own position. They would have to be re-assessed as adopters rather than foster carers. They would lose the support of their fostering officer as well as Darren's social worker. They would be entitled to adoption support services, but these are not as extensive as fostering support. They would also lose their fostering allowance. Adoption allowances can be paid but they are limited to maintenance, without a professional fee, so that would have an impact on the family's finances.

Adoption would also change the composition of their own family: for example, Darren would gain the same inheritance rights as Ivan. And, much as Darren thinks it would be good not to be in care any more, he would lose out on his leaving care rights.

They also think about Enid. She accepts Darren staying permanently, but she is very unlikely to agree to not be his mum any more. Geoff and Hazel would end up in a legal battle with Enid, jeopardising all the hard work that brought them to their current understanding.

All things considered, Geoff, Hazel and Darren think that adoption is a step too far.

Concurrent planning

There are some specialist 'concurrent planning' schemes under which a child (usually a baby or very young child) is placed with carers who are approved both as foster carers and adopters. The child is initially placed with the family as foster carers while a committed attempt is made to rehabilitate the child home. However, if rehabilitation fails, the child remains with the same carers who shift in status to prospective adopters, avoiding a change of placement and disrupted attachments.

Concurrent planning requires very careful and expert work, and specially selected families who can commit fully to working to return a child home while at the same time being committed to the same child becoming a permanent, full member of their family through adoption.

Concurrent planning should not be confused with 'twin-track' or 'parallel' planning when social workers explore different options (rehabilitation, family placement or permanence) during care proceedings but it is not planned from the start that the foster family will adopt the child if rehabilitation fails.

Residence orders

Residence orders are at the other end of the scale from adoption. Made under s8 CA89, residence orders simply determine according to the child's best interests whom the child should live with. They give PR to the person with residence, shared with anyone else who already has it. Other than the question of where the child lives, everyone with PR has an equal say in making decisions for the child. Unlike adoption, a residence order does not change family relationships, lasts only to 18 and can be varied or revoked by the court. Additional orders can be made according to the child's best interests – for example, changing the child's surname, regulating contact or restricting applications to vary or revoke the order.

> Geoff and Hazel consider whether a residence order would be a good idea for Darren. It would ensure that he stays with them and bring the mixed blessing of ending the care order, getting rid of social workers and reviews but missing out on leaving care services. It would not skew family relationships like adoption but it would still mean that the couple would cease to be foster carers,

losing their fostering officer and fostering allowance. Residence order allowances are purely discretionary and never include a professional fee.

Under a residence order Geoff and Hazel would gain PR, but this would be shared equally with Enid, so they would have to work directly with her without having the social worker as an intermediary.

Geoff and Hazel decide that a residence order has more disadvantages than advantages and is not for them.

Special Guardianship Orders (SGOs)

SGOs were introduced some time after the rest of CA89 to provide an option that is stronger than a residence order but less drastic than adoption. An SGO does not terminate parents' PR and does not skew family relationships, but it is more secure than a residence order because it cannot easily be revoked or varied. It is stronger than a residence order because, although PR is shared, the special guardian can make decisions without consulting others with PR.

> Geoff and Hazel prefer the option of an SGO to both adoption and residence. Unlike adoption it would not change Darren's legal identity or cut off his legal links with his mother, sister and extended family, nor would it change the composition of the couple's own family. But unlike a residence order, it would give them the authority to make decisions for Darren without having to involve Enid at every stage. They are more likely to get an allowance (still without a professional fee) and support under an SGO than a residence order, but they still lose their status as foster carers and the support of their fostering officer.
>
> Darren is happy that an SGO would get him out of care, get rid of his social worker and ensure that he stays with Geoff and Hazel without cutting his mum out of his life. Enid would retain PR and her status as Darren's mum, and she would be more likely to accept an SGO than adoption.
>
> Geoff and Hazel's lawyer writes to Borsetshire saying that, before seeking an SGO, they need an enforceable written contract agreeing to pay their legal fees for an application, to pay an SGO allowance of at least the level of fostering maintenance allowance, and to provide Darren with the same services into independence as if he had remained in care so that he is not disadvantaged by his change in status.

Applications against local authority plans

The starting point is that foster carers are there to do a professional job on the local authority's behalf. They contribute to decisions for looked after children but they do not make those decisions and, in general, should not be allowed to disrupt plans by making their own applications.

However, the law also recognises that local authorities do not always get things right and a carer who has looked after a child for some time should be entitled to apply to court. The compromise the law sets, therefore, is to allow applications by foster carers even without the local authority's agreement after they have cared for a child for one year, or if the court gives permission to apply.

You will need urgent, detailed and expert legal advice if you want to go ahead without the local authority's support, particularly if you need to stop the child being moved at short notice. Bear in mind that the local authority will of course be able to put its case to the court, and just because an application can go ahead does not mean that it will succeed.

Point for practice

If you are asked to consider a change of legal status for your fostered child, make sure you understand the different legal options. Take legal advice.

Chapter 18

Moving to Independence

Leaving care

We often talk about leaving care or 'after-care' services. In fact, the legal provisions apply to all looked after children whether they are in care or voluntarily accommodated. The key statute is the Children (Leaving Care) Act 2000.

We know that former looked after children often do less well than their counterparts in educational attainment, employment and relationships in adult life. This may be partly due to the complications causing them to be looked after in the first place, but it hardly helps vulnerable young people to send them off on their own into the world at 16 or 18. In recent years, the crucial importance of the transition to independence has been recognised, resulting in a plethora of well-intentioned but sometimes confusing legislation, guidance and initiatives.

Carers have a vital role to play in helping young people move into adulthood – teaching self-care and life skills, boosting self-esteem, supporting education and ambitions and advocating for them. Ask for any training you need on preparing a young person for adult life, the benefits system, housing options or anything else to help you perform your role.

Pathway planning

Before a suitable plan can be devised, young people's needs, skills and goals must be assessed within three months of their 16th birthday. This assessment considers their needs for advice, assistance and support while they are still looked after and beyond. The assessment covers:

- physical, mental and emotional health and development – what the young people need to ensure a healthy future, including advice on sexual health, drugs and on forming healthy relationships

- financial needs, including learning budgeting

- accommodation needs

- education, training and employment needs

- support from family and friends including continuing support from current carers when they move on

- self-care and independent living skills – practical things like cooking and cleaning, and personal skills like assertiveness.

Informed by the assessment, the pathway plan is an agreement between the local authority and the young person to decide the way forward towards independence. Planning must of course be done on an individual basis, taking into account the young person's racial, cultural and linguistic background, any disabilities or other special needs, religion, sexuality and any other relevant characteristics.

The young person should be actively involved in drawing up the plan, which includes:

- a programme to develop skills for independent living

- where the young person will live when moving on from foster care

- the personal support and contact that will be available

- education, training and help to find employment

- support to develop and maintain personal and family relationships

- financial support

- meeting health needs

- a contingency plan.

If, despite every effort, it proves impossible to engage the young person, the local authority still has a statutory duty to draw up a plan. Depending on circumstances and the young person's wishes, parents may also be actively involved.

Pathway planning should look positively at what the young person wants to do and achieve in adulthood. It should be a process, not an event, and kept under regular review, at least every six months and whenever requested by the young person. Foster carers should be actively involved in planning – after all, they often know the young person best of all.

Personal adviser

The personal adviser gives the young person advice, support and information, keeps in touch and keeps up to date with progress. The personal adviser must be involved in drawing up the pathway plan, liaise with the local authority to ensure that promised services are delivered, and be involved in reviews. Although the personal adviser is often specifically appointed to the job by the local authority (in England, often from the Connexions service), there is no reason why a foster carer cannot fulfil that role, if that is what the young person wishes.

Young people's entitlements

There is a rather confusing range of definitions – young people may be:

- 'eligible' (16 or 17 and still looked after)

- 'relevant' (16 or 17, no longer looked after)

- 'former relevant' (18–21-year-olds who were 'eligible' or 'relevant')

- 'qualifying' (under 21s who left care when over 16 but were not 'eligible' or 'relevant').

ELIGIBLE CHILDREN

'Eligible children' are aged 16 or 17, are currently looked after and have been so for at least 13 weeks since the age of 14. They have continuing entitlements as looked after children and must also have a needs assessment, pathway plan and personal adviser.

> Jenny is 16. She was in care from the age of 8 to the age of 13, when her foster carers obtained a residence order for her, discharging the care order. No-one thought about after-care services at the time.

Jenny is not an 'eligible child' because she was too young when she left care. She does not get after-care services.

Keira is 16 and has been in foster care since she was accommodated by Borsetshire when she was 14. She is an 'eligible child'. She has:

- an assessment

- a pathway plan, informed by the assessment, setting out how her needs are to be met and what services are to be provided, by whom and when as she moves from being looked after to becoming independent

- a personal adviser.

RELEVANT CHILDREN

'Relevant children' are 16- and 17-year-olds who are not currently looked after but who were looked after for at least 13 weeks since the age of 14 including some time after the age of 16. Like their 'eligible' counterparts, they are entitled to a needs assessment, pathway plan and personal adviser, but they are also entitled to suitable accommodation and maintenance, and help to achieve pathway goals including assistance in education, training or employment.

'Relevant children' are not usually entitled to claim benefits (unless they are lone parents or are sick or disabled) so depend on their local authority for financial support. How this is actually delivered may vary from one young person to another; some are ready to manage their own budget, while others are not, so the authority handles key expenditure on their behalf.

The local authority must keep in touch and carry on trying to make contact if they lose touch.

Keira is now 17. Her mother discharges her from accommodation (with Keira's agreement – she could legally refuse to go). Keira is a 'relevant child' – she was looked after beyond the age of 14 including time after 16 but she is not looked after now. She has already had an assessment, has a pathway plan and personal adviser. Borsetshire must now keep in touch with her, ensure she has suitable accommodation and maintain her (because she cannot claim benefits). It must help her to achieve the goals in her pathway plan, including cash payments to help her with her college course.

Keira remains with her mother successfully for six months. At that point, she ceases to be a 'relevant child'. Unfortunately their relationship breaks down a couple of months later. As she is still under 18, she reverts to being a 'relevant child'.

FORMER RELEVANT CHILDREN

Anyone between 18 and 21 who used to be a 'relevant' or 'eligible' child is a 'former relevant child'. The local authority must keep in touch. The young person's pathway plan must still be kept under review and the young person still has a personal adviser. A 'former relevant child' is entitled to assistance for education and welfare. These duties continue beyond 21 if the young person remains in education or training.

QUALIFYING CHILDREN

These are young people who were over 16 when they stopped being looked after but did not fulfil the 13-week criterion. The local authority must keep in touch, advise, assist and befriend them and help them with education and training up to the age of 24, including providing or helping out with accommodation out of term-time.

Young people with disabilities

Moving to adulthood can be particularly challenging for young people with disabilities who might have extra difficulties securing accessible accommodation, finding employment or tackling discrimination. Extra government funding is available to improve services for young care-leavers with disabilities.

Especially crucial is the liaison between children's and adults' services. Carers need to make sure that adult services are fully involved in planning at an early stage. In England, Connexions can continue to work with young people with disabilities until they are 25, if they are not ready before then to access adult services.

A particular problem faces young people with a disability or disorder that does not meet eligibility criteria for adult services but who are more vulnerable and less able than others to cope with independent living at an early age. Carers need to be prepared to advocate strongly to ensure that these young people are not further disadvantaged.

Asylum seekers

Young asylum seekers who entered the country as unaccompanied minors may have to face the additional challenge of their unresolved immigration and asylum status. Preparation for adulthood may include preparation for a return to their country of origin. Contact with the National Asylum Support Service and Refugee Council and access to specialist legal advice are vital aspects of planning for them.

Right 2B Cared 4 Pilots

These aim to increase young people's active participation in planning. No significant changes are to be made without a proper review meeting and there are strengthened roles for IROs and the young people themselves, supported by an independent advocate of their own choosing. An effective disputes resolution mechanism is an important part of the scheme. It is anticipated that the scheme will be rolled out nationwide in due course.

Staying Put

Young people living with their own families rarely leap straight from family life into independence at 16 or 18; it is usually a gradual process, the young people moving on when they are ready, not when they hit a certain age – many of us still 'come home to mum' well into adulthood.

For years, foster carers have been providing ongoing support and sometimes unfunded placements for former foster children. Some local authorities allow a placement to continue by changing it from foster care to 'supported lodgings'. Now at last, the 'Staying Put' pilot in England is trying to work out how family placements can continue beyond the age of 18 on a nationwide, formal and funded basis.[1] It is addressing issues including tax and benefits, training, recruitment and managing resources (including implications for younger children needing foster care). There is also the question of legal status to be sorted out.

The National Leaving Care Standards[2] say that local authorities should ensure that young people have the right to remain in care until 18 and the right to stay in their foster or residential placement until they are 21.

---

1   Pilot schemes running in ten local authority areas May 2008–March 2011.
2   Available at www.leavingcare.org/professionals/national_standards_in_leaving_care, accessed on 6 July 2010.

There is clear momentum for change, and in future we can expect young people's legal rights to be strengthened.

Independent living

Local authorities, working jointly with housing associations, should have a range of safe and suitable supported accommodation for young people moving on to independence (bed and breakfast is not acceptable), and there should always be a contingency plan – a plan B in case plan A does not work out.

Young people should receive a grant to set up home. They and their carers should receive a clear written statement in advance setting out exactly what financial support is available.

Representations and complaints

The local authority must have a procedure for representations, including complaints by young people who are entitled to after-care services. This must include access to an independent advocate (s26A CA89).

Points for practice

- Make sure that planning for a fostered child's long-term future starts well before the age of 16.

- Be as clear as you can about your young person's legal entitlements and be prepared to advocate on his behalf.

- Seek training and advice.

Jargon Buster

Acceptable Behaviour Contract (ABC) A voluntary written agreement aiming to divert a child of any age from anti-social behaviour.

Accommodation A voluntary arrangement for the local authority to look after a child (s20 CA89). Parent(s) retain full PR.

Achieving Best Evidence (ABE) Guidelines for interviewing children and other vulnerable witnesses.

Adoption order A court order (Adoption and Children Act 2002) making a child fully and permanently a member of a new family.

Advocate In court – the lawyer who presents a case in court.
In other contexts – a person who speaks up for someone and makes sure their views are heard.

Affirmation A non-religious promise to tell the truth as a witness in court.

Aggravation Factors in a criminal case making an offence more serious.

Anti-Social Behaviour Order (ASBO) A civil order prohibiting specified behaviour that causes or is likely to cause harassment, alarm or distress.

Appropriate adult (AA) A competent adult who is to protect the interests of a young or vulnerable person under arrest (Police and Criminal Evidence Act 1984, Code C).

Area authority The local authority for the area where foster carers live.

Bail Conditional or unconditional release pending a criminal court hearing.

Barrister A lawyer who specialises in advocacy. Only barristers can act in the Crown Court, where they wear wigs and gowns.

British Association for Adoption and Fostering (BAAF) A voluntary organisation that provides advice and resources on adoption and fostering and operates the IRM (in England).

Burden of proof The principle that decides whose job it is to prove the case: in a criminal case, the burden lies on the prosecution; in a civil case, the burden lies on the applicant.

Care and Social Services Inspectorate in Wales (CSSIW) The government agency that inspects fostering agencies in Wales.

Care order A court order (s31 CA89) placing a child in local authority care until the age of 18 (unless the court replaces or discharges the care order later). The local authority gains PR and can override the parents' wishes.

Care plan The plan presented to the court by the local authority containing proposals for a child if a care order is granted.
The ongoing plan for a looked after child (accommodated or in care).

Care proceedings The court case in which a local authority applies for a care order.

Care Standards Act 2000 The statute governing fostering agencies.

Case conference A multi-agency meeting that determines whether a child is at continuing risk of significant harm and whether he should be made subject to a 'child protection plan'.

Case law Law that is decided by the higher courts (Court of Appeal and House of Lords/ Supreme Court), setting a precedent that all other courts must follow in similar cases.

Case Management Conference (CMC) One of the standard court hearings in care proceedings when the court fixes the timetable for the case and orders statements to be filed.

Caution First meaning: the police caution to a suspect on arrest and before questioning, explaining the right to silence.
Second meaning: an alternative to an adult being charged and tried with an offence.

Charge The precise criminal offence of which a defendant is accused.

Child protection plan The plan devised by a case conference for a child at risk of significant harm, designed to eliminate, reduce or manage the risk. The list of children subject to child protection plans replaced the Child Protection Register.

Child Safety Order (CSO) An order available for children under ten who act in a way that would be a crime or anti-social behaviour if they were older.

Children Act 1989 (CA89) The main statute dealing with children's welfare, child protection and care proceedings.

Children and Family Courts Advisory and Support Service (CAFCASS) The organisation that employs Children's Guardians.

Children Panel An accreditation scheme for solicitors with proven expertise in children law cases.

Children's Guardian A CAFCASS officer appointed by the court to represent a child's interests in care or adoption proceedings.

Clerk to the Justices The legally qualified adviser to the magistrates, who advises them on the law and procedure.

Closed question A question that limits the possible answers (e.g. 'Was it Mummy or Daddy who hit you?').

Code C The guidance detailing how suspects must be treated by the police at the police station (issued under the Police and Criminal Evidence Act 1984).

Concurrent planning A special project in which a child is placed with a family who foster a child with a view to rehabilitation but, if that fails, will adopt the child.

Contact Contact between a child and another person – ranging from indirect contact (e.g. letters, photos) to visiting and staying.

Contact order A court order (s8 CA89 or s34 CA89 if the child is in care) determining what contact (if any) is to be arranged between a child and a named person.

County Court A court in which a judge hears family cases. It is more senior and hears more complicated cases than the FPC.

Court of Appeal A very senior court, which hears appeals from decisions from lower courts. The Court of Appeal's decisions decide the law for all lower courts.

Criminal Injuries Compensation Authority (CICA) The government agency that awards compensation to victims of crime.

Criminal Records Bureau (CRB) The government agency that certifies an individual's record of criminal convictions, cautions and (in an enhanced check) other relevant information.

Cross-examination The opponent's advocate's questions to a witness designed to test or undermine the witness's evidence.

Crown Court A court in which a judge and jury hear serious criminal cases.

Crown Prosecution Service (CPS) The government agency that conducts prosecutions in the name of the Crown.

Data Protection Act (DPA) 1998 Legislation regulating the safekeeping, handling and disclosure of personal information.

Department for Children, Schools and Families (DCSF) The government department now superceded by the Department for Education.

Department for Education (DfE) The government department headed by the Secretary of State responsible for all policies involving children in England (replacing the DCSF from May 2010).

Disposal The final resolution in a court case – making an order or no order in family proceedings, giving a discharge or passing a sentence in a criminal case.

Eligible child A term used in defining rights to after-care services referring to 16- or 17-year-olds who are looked after.

Emergency Protection Order (EPO) A short-term order (s44 CA89) authorising a child's immediate removal to a safe place if the court is satisfied that he will suffer significant harm if he is not removed. The order can be made without the parents' knowledge. It confers PR.

European Convention on Human Rights A convention defining fundamental human rights and freedoms, made part of UK law by the Human Rights Act 1998.

European Court of Human Rights The ultimate court of appeal on questions of human rights sitting in Strasbourg.

Every Child Matters A DCSF programme aiming to achieve five outcomes for all children: being healthy, staying safe, enjoying and achieving, making a positive contribution, achieving economic well-being.

Evidence The information a court takes into account in making its decision. Evidence can be in writing, given orally or both.

Examination in chief Questions asked by the advocate who called the witness.

Family Proceedings Court (FPC) The section of the Magistrates' Court that hears family cases. All care proceedings start in the FPC and many remain there throughout.

Former relevant child A term used in defining rights to after-care services, referring to 18–21-year-olds who were looked after.

Foster care agreement The agreement setting out the relationship between agency and carer (not concerning a particular placement).

Foster placement agreement or placement plan The detailed agreement between carers and placing authority about the placement of a particular child.

Fostering agency A fostering service operated by a local authority or IFA.

Fostering panel A panel established by a fostering agency to make recommendations about approval, terms and termination of approval of foster carers.

Hearsay Second-hand evidence. Criminal courts cannot accept hearsay evidence; family courts and courts hearing applications for ASBOs can.

High Court (Family Division) A senior court, which hears very complicated family cases and also appeals from the FPC.

House of Lords This used to be the highest court in the land, and has now been replaced by the Supreme Court.

Human Rights Act 1998 The Act guaranteeing fundamental human rights in all areas of the law, and giving individuals the right to apply to court if their rights are breached.

Independent fostering agency (IFA) A fostering agency operated by an individual, partnership, company or charitable organisation registered under the Care Standards Act 2000.

Independent Review Mechanism (IRM) The procedure in England for an independent panel to make a recommendation about an agency's proposal to refuse, change the terms of or refuse approval as a foster carer.

Independent Reviewing Officer (IRO) A qualified and experienced person who chairs reviews for looked after children and ensures that care plans are put into action.

Independent Safeguarding Authority (ISA) The government body that administers the vetting and barring scheme for people working with children and vulnerable adults.

Individual Support Order (ISO) A civil order imposing positive requirements designed to tackle the causes of anti-social behaviour, often coupled with an ASBO.

Interim Care Order (ICO) An order placing a child in local authority care for a limited time (usually four weeks) while care proceedings are underway.

Issue Resolution Hearing (IRH) One of the standard hearings in care proceedings when the court ensures that the case is ready for a final hearing.

Judge A qualified and experienced lawyer who decides family cases or who presides in the Crown Court, deciding on procedure, law and sentencing.

Lawyer A general term for a legal professional – solicitor, barrister, legal executive or academic.

Leading question A question that indicates the required answer (e.g. 'It was Daddy who hit you, wasn't it?').

Legal Aid State funding of legal fees for people involved in court cases. All parents and children involved in care proceedings automatically receive free Legal Aid.

Local Authority Designated Officer (LADO) The key officer in allegations against adults working with children, responsible for advice, liaison and monitoring procedures.

Local Safeguarding Children Board (LSCB) The high level multi-agency body (including health, education, children's social care and police) responsible for inter-agency working and local policies.

Looked after child A child who is looked after by the local authority voluntarily (s20 CA89), under a care order (s31 CA89) or via the criminal justice system.

Magistrate A lay Justice of the Peace or a professional District Judge (Magistrates' Court). Magistrates hear adult criminal cases and some sit in the FPC and Youth Court.

Mitigation Factors reducing the seriousness of a criminal offence.

National Minimum Standards for Fostering Government-recommended minimum standards for fostering agencies against which agencies are inspected.

Oath Swearing on the Bible or other religious book to tell the truth when giving evidence in court.

Official Solicitor A government appointee representing interests of adults who are not capable of understanding court proceedings they are involved in (through youth, learning disabilities or mental health problems).

Ofsted The body that inspects fostering agencies in England.

Open question A question that allows the respondent to answer freely (e.g. 'What happened?').

Parental responsibility (PR) The power and responsibility to make decisions for a child.

Parenting order An order making parents attend counselling or guidance, or imposing conditions on the care of their child if the child is convicted of a criminal offence, given an ASBO or a CSO.

Party to proceedings A person who is directly involved in court proceedings, entitled to be present in court, have all the evidence, give evidence, call witnesses and be represented by a lawyer.

Pathway plan A plan drawn up following an assessment to plan a young person's transition from being looked after to independence.

Personal Education Plan (PEP) Plan setting out how a looked after child is to be enabled to meet his educational potential.

Personal Health Plan (PHP) Plan setting out how a looked after child's health needs are to be met.

Placement order An order (Adoption and Children Act 2002) giving a local authority the right to place a child for adoption.

Placing authority The local authority legally responsible for a child placed in foster care.

Plea The defendant's formal declaration of whether he is guilty or not guilty.

Police and Criminal Evidence Act 1984 (PACE) The key legislation governing the treatment and questioning of suspects at the police station.

Police protection The police power (s46 CA89) to remove a child immediately to a safe place if he will suffer significant harm if he is not removed. This administrative power does not involve the court.

Precedent A case decided by the Court of Appeal or Supreme Court, which determines the law on a particular issue.

Pre-sentence reports Court-ordered reports (e.g. YOT, probation or psychiatric reports) where the defendant has pleaded or been found guilty to help determine the appropriate sentence.

Presumption of innocence A person is innocent of an offence unless and until proven guilty.

Private fostering An arrangement made between individuals for one person to look after another's child. A private foster carer is not approved by a fostering agency and the child is not 'looked after'.

Private law Family disputes involving individuals, such as residence or contact disputes.

Public law Children's cases involving the local authority, (e.g. care proceedings).

Public Law Outline (PLO) The procedural guidelines for the conduct of care proceedings cases.

Qualifying child A term used in defining rights to after-care services, referring to under 21-year-olds who were looked after but are not 'eligible' or 'relevant'.

Re-examination Questions from the advocate who called the witness following up from cross-examination.

Referral order A sentence available on a first conviction and guilty plea. A Youth Offender Panel decides what requirements are imposed, including elements of restorative justice.

Register of Foster Carers A list of its approved foster carers maintained by each fostering agency.

Relevant child A term used in defining rights to after-care services – referring to 16- and 17-year-olds who are no longer looked after.

Remand Where bail is refused, remand determines restrictions on the defendant's liberty pending criminal trial. Young defendants are usually remanded to local authority accommodation.

Reprimand An alternative to prosecution for a first-time young offender who admits guilt.

Residence order A court order (s8 CA89) deciding whom a child lives with. That person has PR.

Responsible authority The local authority that has a care order for a child or that is accommodating him.

Restorative justice Sentencing options designed to encourage the offender to take responsibility, make reparation and reintegrate into society. Victims may be directly involved.

Section 7 report A social work report advising the court on a child's welfare in private law proceedings (s7 CA89).

Section 8 order Residence, contact, specific issue and prohibited steps orders (s8 CA89).

Section 34(4) order An order allowing a local authority to refuse contact between a named person and a child in care (s34[4] CA89).

Section 37 report A report ordered by a court in private law proceedings when the court believes that care proceedings might be appropriate (s37 CA89).

Section 47 enquiry A child protection enquiry carried out after a referral to children's social care.

Secure accommodation order A court order authorising a local authority to place a child in locked accommodation on welfare grounds (s25 CA89) or a requirement on remand.

Secure training centre (STC) A form of custody for offenders up to age 17.

Sentence The punishment imposed by the court on a convicted offender.

Significant harm The key term in child protection including physical, emotional and sexual harm through abuse or neglect, or seeing or hearing someone else being abused.

Solicitor A lawyer who sees clients, prepares cases and may also conduct advocacy in some courts.

Special Guardianship Order (SGO) A court order (s14A CA89) appointing a special guardian who has PR for a child and can make decisions without consulting the parents.

Specific Issue Order A court order (s8 CA89) determining a particular question about the exercise of parental responsibility

Standard of proof The degree of certainty required for a court to decide that a case is proven. In criminal cases the standard is 'beyond reasonable doubt'; in family cases it is 'on the balance of probabilities'.

Statute Law made by Parliament – also called legislation or Acts of Parliament.

Supervision order A court order (s31 CA89) ordering the local authority to advise, assist and befriend the child for up to one year (extension possible up to three years in total). The authority does not obtain PR.

Supreme Court The highest court in the land (replacing the House of Lords from October 2009). It hears appeals on cases of general public importance. Its decisions determine the law of the land and are binding on all other courts.

Test case A case taken to court to decide a controversial question of legal interpretation, seeking to set a binding precedent.

Threshold criteria The grounds the local authority must prove to obtain a care or supervision order (s31 CA89) – actual or likely significant harm due to the child receiving inadequate care or being beyond parental control.

Twin-tracking Assessing different possible care plans (e.g. return home or adoption) at the same time during care proceedings.

Verdict Finding the defendant in a criminal trial 'guilty' or 'not guilty'.

Warning An alternative to prosecution for a young offender – in between a reprimand and charge.

Welfare checklist A list of factors the family court must consider in deciding which order, if any, to make in a child's best interests (s1(3) CA89).

Welfare principle The child's welfare is the family court's paramount consideration (s1(1) CA89).

Witness A person who provides evidence to the court.

Working Together Government guidance for multi-agency working in child protection.

Young offenders' institution (YOI) Equivalent to prison for older teenagers and young adult offenders aged up to 20.

Youth Court The section of the Magistrates' Court dealing with criminal charges against defendants aged under 18.

Youth Offending Team (YOT) A multi-agency team with statutory duties playing a key role in youth justice.

Youth Rehabilitation Order (YRO) A community sentence allowing the court to impose any combination of 18 possible requirements to fit the crime and the offender.

Resources

The full text of Acts of Parliament and Regulations are all available on the Office of Public Sector Information website – www.opsi.gov.uk.

Adoption
Adoption and Children Act 2002

Care planning
Care Planning, Placement and Case Review Regulations 2010
Independent Reviewing Officers – www.dcsf.gov.uk/everychildmatters/
    safeguardingandsocialcare/childrenincare/independentreviewingofficers/iro

Care proceedings
CAFCASS (Children and Family Courts Advisory and Support Service) – www.cafcass.gov.uk
CAFCASS Wales – www.wales.gov.uk/cafcasscymru/home/?lang=en
HM Courts Service – www.hmcourts-service.gov.uk
Public Law Outline – www.judiciary.gov.uk/docs/public_law_outline.pdf

Children's welfare and child protection
Care Planning, Placement and Review Regulations (England) 2010
Children Act 1989
Children and Young Persons Act 2008
Department for Children, Schools and Families – www.dcsf.gov.uk
Department for Education – www.education.gov.uk
Welsh National Assembly – www.wales.gov.uk
Working Together to Safeguard Children: A Guide to Inter-Agency Working to Safeguard and Promote the Welfare of Children (DCSF 2010). Available at http://publications.education.gov.uk. Reference: DCSF-00305-2010.

Data protection
Data Protection Act 1998
Information Commissioner – www.ico.gov.uk

Fostering agencies
BAAF – www.baaf.co.uk
Care Standards Act 2000
Care and Social Services Inspectorate (Wales) – www.csiw.wales.gov.uk (inspection agency)
Children's Workforce Development Council – www.cwdcouncil.org.uk (training provider)
Fostering Network – www.fostering.net
Fostering Services Regulations 2002; Fostering Services (Wales) Regulations 2003
Independent Review Mechanism – www.irm-adoption.org.uk/fostering
National Minimum Standards for Fostering (England) – www.dh.gov.uk/en/
    Publicationsandstatistics/Publications/PublicationsPolicyAndGuidance/DH_4005551
    (standards issued in 2002, currently being revised and updated)
National Minimum Standards for Fostering Services (Wales) – www.csiw.wales.gov.uk/docs/
    Standards_Fostering_e.pdf
Ofsted (England) – www.ofsted.gov.uk (inspection agency)

Human rights
Human Rights Act 1998
Liberty – www.liberty-human-rights.org.uk

Leaving care
Children (Leaving Care) Act 2000
Connexions – www.connexions-direct.com
National Care Advisory Service – www.leavingcare.org; www.dcsf.gov.uk/everychildmatters/
    safeguardingandsocialcare/childrenleavingcare

Legal advice
Children Panel accredited solicitors – www.sra.org.uk/solicitors
Children's Legal Centre – www.childrenslegalcentre.com
National Youth Advocacy Service – www.nyas.net

Managing allegations
Fosterline – www.fostering.net/resources/advice/england/fosterline
Protecting Children, Supporting Foster Carers – www.dcsf.gov.uk/everychildmatters/
    resources-and-practice/IG00082

Vetting, barring and police checks
Criminal Records Bureau – www.crb.homeoffice.gov.uk
Independent Safeguarding Authority – www.isa-gov.org.uk

Youth justice

Achieving Best Evidence in Criminal Proceedings: Guidance on Interviewing Victims and Witnesses Using Special Measures – www.cps.gov.uk/Publications/docs/Achieving_Best_Evidence_FINAL.pdf

Crime and Disorder Act 1998

Criminal Injuries Compensation Authority – www.cica.gov.uk

PACE Codes – www.police.homeoffice.gov.uk/operational-policing/powers-pace-codes/pace-code-intro

Police and Criminal Evidence Act 1984

Pre-Trial Therapy for Child Witnesses – www.cps.gov.uk/publications/prosecution/therapychild.html

Witness support – NSPCC – www.nspcc.org.uk/whatwedo/servicesforchildrenandfamilies/YWS/youngwitnesssupport_wda.61880.html

Youth Justice Board – www.yjb.gov.uk/en-gb

Index

Acceptable Behaviour Contract (ABC) 186–7
accommodated child 68, 70, 75–8
  care order, contrast with 83–4
  care plan 118–19
  child's wishes and feelings 78, 119
  contact 133–4
  discharge from 77–8, 122, 220
  duty to accommodate 75–6
  parental responsibility 70, 76–7
Achieving Best Evidence guidelines 194–9
  see also interviews with children
adoption 66, 70, 209, 211–13, 224
  consent to 212
  effect of 70, 83, 211–12, 213
  parental responsibility 70, 72, 211–12
  placement order 95, 212
  procedural safeguards 212
  residence order, in contrast with 214
  special guardianship, in contrast with 215
  step-parent, by 66
affirmation 106, 168, 202
after-care services see leaving care services
agency see fostering agency
aggravation of offences 173
allegations and complaints against carers 23, 54–8
anti-social behaviour 186–90
  diversion from 139, 140, 141
Anti-Social Behaviour Order (ASBO) 140, 141, 187–9
  breach of 189
  contents of 189
  duration of 189
  grounds for 187
  hearsay evidence 187–8

implications of 189
parenting order 141
reporting of 188
special measures for witnesses 188
standard of proof 188
appropriate adult (AA) 153, 154–60
  choice of 154–5
  charge in presence of 164
  reprimand in presence of 162
approval see foster carer approval
area authority 21, 33, 46, 55, 59
arrest 145, 150–1, 152, 156
  caution 145, 151
  right to have someone informed of 152, 156
Article 6 see fair trial
asylum seekers 222
attendance centre 178, 180

BAAF (British Association for Adoption and Fostering) 38
bail 151, 161, 162, 164–5
  breach of 165
  conditions 165
  offence committed while on 173
  refusal of 165, 166
balance of probabilities 94, 143, 147, 188
  criminal standard, in contrast with 143
  Criminal Injuries Compensation Scheme 204
balanced evidence 102–3, 104
beyond reasonable doubt 143, 145, 147
  ASBO 188
  civil standard, in contrast with 143
burden of proof 143

CAFCASS 60, 68, 89–90, 92, 124
  see also Children's Guardian
Care and Social Services Inspectorate in Wales (CSSIW) 21, 55
care order 75, 78, 81–4
  care plan 94, 117
  contact 83
  in contrast with accommodation 83–4
  in contrast with supervision order 9
  discharge of 122, 126, 211, 214, 215
  duration of 83
  effects of 83–4
  grounds for 81
  looked after child 75
  parental responsibility 66, 68, 69, 83–4
care plan 82, 117–20
  accommodated child 118–19
  care order 82, 94, 117–18
  contingency plan 117, 119
  education plan see Personal Education Plan
  health plan see Personal Health Plan
  legal action to enforce 124–7
  review of see reviews
Care Planning, Placement and Case Review Regulations 112, 119
care proceedings 69, 86–98
  application by local authority 86, 88, 92
  Case Management Conference 92
  child's role in 89–91
  courts 87–8
  criminal proceedings, in relation to 143, 147
  Issue Resolution Hearing 92
  interim hearings 93

care proceedings *cont.*
  final hearing 93, 94
  foster carer's role in 96–7
  parties to 88
  Public Law Outline 86–7,
    92–3
  procedure 92–4
  respondents to 88
  stages in 92–3
  statement 103–4
Care Standards Act 2000 19, 21
Case Management Conference *see*
    care proceedings
case record 24, 35, 54
caution
  for offence 28
  police caution 145, 146, 151,
    156, 164
changing agencies 59–60
child in care 78
  see also care order; care
    proceedings; looked after
    child
child protection
  case conference 79–80
  investigations 55, 57, 79, 193
  plan, child subject to 79
Child Safety Order (CSO) 140–1
Children Act 1989 (CA89) 65, 139
  s3(5) 71
  s7 *see* Section 7 report
  s8 *see* private law
  s20 *see* accommodated child
  s31 *see* care order
  s34, s34(4) *see* contact
  s37 *see* Section 37 report
Children and Young Persons Act
    2008 112, 114
Children (Leaving Care) Act 2000
    217
Children Panel solicitor 90, 211
  see also solicitor for the child
Children's Guardian 89–90, 92, 96,
    97, 135, 147
children's guide 22, 50
Children's Workforce Development
    Council 29, 48
Codes *see* Police and Criminal
    Evidence Act 1984
communication aids 203
community orders *see* sentencing
competence of young person 73
  to instruct solicitor 91
complaints
  allegations against carers 23,
    54–8
  local authority procedure 24,
    124, 223
concurrent planning 214
confidentiality 34, 43, 47, 49,
    50–1, 52, 99,
  of placement 106, 115

consent
  to medical treatment *see* medical
    treatment
  to placement 40–1
contact 44, 47, 128–36
  accommodated child 133–4
  child in care 83, 132
  child's welfare 128
  child's wishes and feelings 135
  considerations in arranging
    129
  court's duty to consider 94
  duty to promote 22, 134
  foster carer's role in 44
  indirect contact 130
  long-term placement and
    209–10
  order
    child's application for 135
    s34 CA89 83, 118, 132–3
    s8 CA89 44, 68, 69,
      133–4
  purpose of 128–9
  refusal of 83, 132–3
  right to 132
  siblings, with 134, 135
  supervision of 130–1
Connexions 219, 221
corporal punishment 34
County Court *see* court
court
  County Court 87, 92, 106,
    143, 147
  Crown Court 143, 145–6,
    147, 172, 203
    procedures in 169–70
  Family Proceedings Court
    (FPC) 87, 106, 140, 147
  High Court 87, 88, 106
  Magistrates Court 87, 145,
    146, 151, 167, 188
    preparing for 104–5
  Youth Court 145–6, 147, 154,
    167–9, 171, 172, 188
    press and public in 169
    procedures in 167–8
    trial in 168–9
crime
  Crime and Disorder Act 1998
    139, 141
  investigation of 153–4
  meaning of 142
  prevention of 139–40
criminal charge 161, 163–4
Criminal Injuries Compensation
    204–6
criminal intention 142, 172
criminal proceedings
  care proceedings, in relation to
    143, 147
  foster carer's role in 170

Criminal Records Bureau (CRB) 26,
    28–9, 163, 179
criminal responsibility 72, 140–1
cross-examination 106, 108–9, 168
  of child witness 199, 202–203
Crown Court *see* court
Crown Prosecution Service (CPS)
    141, 164, 167, 168, 200
cultural heritage *see* diversity
curfew 180–1
custody
  conditions of 156–7
  custodial sentence 175, 183–4
  record 152, 155

Data Protection Act 1998 (DPA)
    24, 51–2
detention
  and training order 183–4
  at Her Majesty's pleasure 183
  without charge 151
disability 20, 43, 73, 114, 198,
    218, 221
discharge 175
disclosure 103, 191–4
diversity 49, 112, 114–15, 122,
    218
  agency's duty to consider 23
  assessment of foster carers
    27–8
  cultural issues in interviewing
    children 194
  decision making 114–15
  matching 40, 114–15
  pathway plan 218
  recruitment of foster carers 114
  reviews 122
  training of foster carers 114
  welfare checklist 82
drug testing 153

education *see* Personal Education
    Plan 43, 117, 119–20
eligible child 219–20
emergency placements 46–7
Emergency Protection Order (EPO)
    46, 66, 78, 80–1, 86
European Court of Human Rights
    144
evidence
  expert 101
  hearsay 146, 187–8
  opinion 100–2
  oral 105–9
  rules of criminal 146
  statement 103
  video interview as 199
examination in chief 106, 108
expert assessment 93–4

factitious or induced illness 88
fair trial 125, 144
family life, right to respect for
    (Article 8) 128–9, 210
Family Proceedings Court (FPC)
    see court
final hearing see care proceedings
final warning 161, 162–3
fine 175
Form F 27
former relevant child 219, 221
foster care agreement 33–5, 44
foster carer
    allegation against 54–8
    application against local
        authority by 216
    approval 33–4
        variation of terms 53
    approval notice 33
    assessment 25, 26–9, 30
    barred persons 25–6, 28
    changing agency 59–60
    child's disclosure to 191–3
    convictions and cautions 28
    diary 97, 99–103
        contents of 100
        importance of balance
            102–3
        factual records 100–1
    evidence to court 99
    induction training 36
    information to 50–1
    parental responsibility and 66,
        70, 209
    payments to see fostering
        allowance
    resigning as carer 59–60
    retiring 59
    review of approval 53–4
    role in care proceedings 96–7
    role in criminal proceedings
        170
    supervising contact 130–1
    supervision 52
    support 45, 48, 52
        during investigation 56
    termination of approval 58, 60
    training and development 23,
        29, 36, 48–9
    transfer protocol 59–60
    unsuccessful application 36–9
    variation of terms of approval
        53
foster placement agreement 42–5,
    119
fostering agency
    agreements with placing
        authority 42
    allegations against carers 54–6
    children's guide 22, 50
    complaints procedure 23
    decisions 33, 36, 38, 60

discipline policy 23
    duties 22–4
    handbook 23, 36, 50
    independent fostering agency
        (IFA) 20–1
    legal provisions 19–20, 21
    meaning of 20
    panel see fostering panel
    policies and procedures 23, 50
    records 24, 35–6, 39, 45
    registered manager 22
    registration and inspection
        of 21
    representations to 36, 37,
        53, 60
    responsible person 22
    restraint 23
    staff 22
    statement of purpose 22, 50
    transfer of carers 59–60
fostering allowance 43, 52–3, 55,
    60, 213, 214
Fostering Network 26, 59
fostering panel 30–3, 36, 60
    meetings 32–3
    membership 31–2
    role 30–1
    recommendations 33, 36, 60
Fostering Services Regulations 19,
    21, 33, 34, 46
    Schedule 3 26
Fosterline 58

'Gillick competence' 73
Guardian see Children's Guardian
guilty plea 143
    credit for 174
    referral order 176
guilty verdict 143, 171

health care 43, 119
health plan see Personal Health Plan
hearsay 146, 187–8
Hedley J 79
High Court see court
Human Rights Act 1998 116, 128,
    131, 142, 149, 210
    breach of 126–7

identification 154
Independent Fostering Agency
    (IFA) see fostering agency
independent living 223
Independent Review Mechanism
    (IRM) 36–9, 60
Independent Reviewing Officer
    (IRO) 44, 69, 122–4, 125,
    126, 127, 135, 210, 222

Independent Safeguarding
    Authority (ISA) 25, 26 28,
    55, 58
independent visitors 135–6
Individual Support Order 189–90
induction training 36
information exchange 41, 50–1, 52
innocence, presumption of 142
intensive fostering see Youth
    Rehabilitation Order
Interim care order (ICO) 66, 78,
    81, 93
interim hearing 93
intermediary 197, 203
interpreter 156, 197
interviews with children
    cultural considerations 194
    foster carer's role 197
    further interviews 198–9
    in court 198
    interpreters and intermediaries
        197
    interviewer 194, 196
    phases 197–198
    preparation for 195–6
    purpose of 195, 199
    questions 198
    interview suite 196
    trained interviewers 192, 196
    video recording of 195, 196,
        199, 202
    see also Achieving Best Evidence
        guidelines
Issue Resolution Hearing see care
    proceedings

joint investigations 57, 193–4, 196
judge 87, 91, 109, 145, 169, 203
judicial review 125, 126
jury 145, 146, 169

LAC reviews 44, 120–2, 123–4,
    210
    frequency of 120–1
    participants in 121
    purpose of 121
    topics covered by 122
    see also Independent Reviewing
        Officer (IRO)
leaving care services 211, 213,
    214, 217–23
    see also eligible child; former
        relevant child; pathway
        plan; relevant child;
        qualifying child
Legal Aid 88, 127
legal advice 152, 156
linguistic heritage see diversity
Local Authority Designated Officer
    (LADO) 54, 56, 57

long-term fostering 209–11
looked after child 75–85, 111–27
    care order 82
    contact with 134
    leaving care / accommodation
        see leaving care services
    local authority duties to 83,
        111–27
    reviews see LAC
    visits to see social work visits

magistrate 87, 109, 146, 167, 188
matching 40–1
medical examination 199–200
medical treatment 43, 67, 73, 84
mitigation 173
Munby LJ 111, 116

National Leaving Care Standards
    222
National Minimum Standards for
    Fostering 20, 21, 56
National Standards for Young
    Witness Preparation 201
negligence 142, 172
not guilty
    plea 143, 166–7, 168, 179
    verdict 143
notification of placement 41–42
NSPCC 201

oath 106, 168, 202
Official Solicitor 88, 124
Ofsted 21, 55
opinions as evidence 100–2
overnight stays 43–4, 210

PACE see Police and Criminal
    Evidence Act 1984 (PACE)
parental responsibility (PR) 65–72
    accommodation 68, 75–7,
        83–4
    adoption 70, 72, 211–12
    care order 66, 68, 69, 83–4
    contact 132, 133, 134
    criminal injuries compensation
        205
    delegation of 70
    emergencies 71
    Emergency Protection Order
        and 81
    ending of 71–2
    fathers 66
    foster carers 66, 70, 209
    medical treatment 43, 67, 84
    mothers 65–6
    non-parents 66
    parties to care proceedings 88

removal of 72
residence order 66, 214–15
sharing 68
special guardianship 215
step-parents 66
supervision order 95
parenting order 140–1
pathway plan 116, 120, 205,
    217–9, 220, 221
permanence 119, 122
    fostering and 210
    legal routes to 211–16
personal adviser 219, 220, 221
Personal Education Plan 119–20,
    122
Personal Health Plan 117, 119,
    122
placement
    children with disabilities 114
    confidential address 115
    consent to 41
    cultural and diversity
        considerations 114
    emergency 46–7
    ending 45, 46
    location of 112
    notification of 41–2
    wishes and feelings
        of child 115
        of parents 116
        of relevant people 116
    supervision of 45
    with siblings 113–14
placement order see adoption
placement plan see foster placement
    agreement
placing authority 34, 40–2, 46, 50,
    52, 54, 55
plea 143, 166
police
    arrest powers 150–1
    identification procedures 154
    interview of suspect 153–4,
        157–8
    interview of witnesses 153
    investigations 55, 57, 153–4
    search of premises 149–50
    search of suspect's person 153
    stop and search 148–9
    station
        obligation to go to 151
        suspect's rights at 152, 156
Police and Criminal Evidence Act
    1984 (PACE) 152, 156
    Code C 153, 154, 156–7
    Code D 154
Police Complaints Commission 149
police protection 80, 86
preparing for court see court
pre-sentence reports 171–2, 179,
    183

private foster care 18
private law orders 68–9, 133–4
    see also contact order; prohibited
        steps order; residence
        order; specific issue order
prohibited steps order 68
Public Law Outline (PLO) 86–7,
    92–3

qualifying child 219, 221

racial and cultural heritage see
    diversity
recklessness 142, 172
record keeping 99–103
re-examination 109
referral order 175, 176–9
    contract under 177
    duration of 176
    effect of 176
    eligibility for 176
    end of 179
    failure to co-operate with 178
    objective of 178
    victim involvement 177
Register of Foster Carers 24, 35, 54
register of fostered children 24, 45
rehabilitation to parents 128
relevant child 219, 220–1
religion see diversity
remand 165–6, 171
    remand fostering 165–6
    secure remands 166
    to local authority
        accommodation 75, 165
reporting restrictions
    ASBOs 188
    Crown Courts 169
    Youth Courts 169
representations, right to make 36,
    37, 53
reprimands 161–3
residence order 66, 68, 69, 118,
    214–15
respondents
    care proceedings 88
responsible authority 21
restorative justice 163, 175, 176,
    186
restraint 23
reviews see foster carer, review of
    approval; LAC reviews
right to remain silent 145
Right 2B Cared 4 pilot 222

Section 7 report 69
Section 8 orders see private law
Section 20 see accommodated child
Section 34 see contact

Section 37 report 69
secure accommodation 140, 166, 184
secure remand 166
secure training centre 184
sentencing 145, 163, 171–85
    aggravation 173
    community orders 175, 176–83
        see also referral order; Youth Rehabilitation Order
    custodial sentence 183–4
    determining sentence 172–5
    discharge 175
    financial penalty 175
    mitigation 173
    objectives of 171
    offender's characteristics 173–4
    pre-sentence reports 171–2, 179, 183
    seriousness of offence 172
    types of sentence 175
    victim impact statement 175
sex offenders register 163
sexuality
    discrimination 38, 39
    interview planning 194
    pathway planning 218
siblings
    contact with 134, 135
    placement with 113–14
significant harm 78–9
    likely to suffer 80, 81
    reasonable cause to suspect 79
    threshold criteria 81, 94
sleep-overs see overnight stays
social work visits 44, 45, 120, 210
solicitor
    Children Panel solicitor 90, 211
    Official Solicitor 88, 124
    solicitor for child 90–1, 96, 97, 135
Special Guardianship order (SGO) 66, 68, 69, 215
special measures
    defendants ineligible for 170
    in ASBO hearings 188
    for child witnesses 170, 191, 202–3
        see also Achieving Best Evidence guidelines; interviewing children
special needs and criminal courts 168
Specific Issue Order 68, 69
standard of proof 143, 188
    see also balance of probabilities; beyond reasonable doubt

statement
    of purpose see foster agency, statement of purpose
    to police 153–154
Statement of Special Educational Needs 43, 120, 125
Staying Put scheme 222–3
stop and search 148–9
strict liability offences 142
supervision
    for carers 52
    of placement 45
    of contact 130–1
    order 95
support for carers 45, 52
suspects' rights 152, 156–7

tagging 165, 166, 178, 181
termination of approval 58, 60
theft 142
therapy before trial 200–1
threshold criteria 79, 94, 95
    see also significant harm
Training, Support and Development Standards for Foster Care 48–9
    see also foster carer, training and development
Transfer of Carers Protocol 59–60
trial, criminal 167, 168–9
TV link evidence 202–3
    see also special measures
twin-track planning 214

Unsuccessful applicants 36–9
'usual fostering limit' 33

verdict 143, 169, 171, 204
vetting and barring scheme 26
victim
    child evidence in court 191
        see also special measures
    compensation see Criminal Injuries Compensation
    involvement in final warning 163
    involvement in referral order 177
    victim impact statement 175
video recorded interviews see interviews with children

Ward LJ 79
welfare
    checklist 81–2, 94
    of child 68, 81, 94, 128, 212
    of defendant
        youth justice system 141, 171

wishes and feelings of child 23, 78, 82, 103, 115, 119, 126
    care proceedings 89, 90
    contact 135
witness
    child 191
        preparation for court 201
        special measures for, see 'Special measures'
        support for 201, 202, 204
    foster carer 99–110
        oral evidence 105–9
        preparation for court 104–5
        statement 103–4, 107
        support 105
    statement to police 153–4
    summons 153
Working Together 55–6, 79

Youth Court see court
Young Offenders Institution (YOI) 165, 184
Youth Offender Panel 176–8
    see also referral order
Youth Offending Team (YOT) 140, 141, 162, 167, 170
    ASBO 187
    assessment by 161
    Child Safety Order 140
    composition of 141
    detention and training order 184
    final warning 163
    intensive fostering 181–2
    pre-sentence report by 171
    referral order 176–8
    reprimand 162
    supervision 165
    Youth Rehabilitation Order 182
Youth Rehabilitation Order 175, 179–83
    breach of 182–3
    eligibility for 179
    intensive fostering 181–2
    intensive supervision and surveillance 181
    requirements under 180–1
    residence requirement 180